# Snakebit!

## WE'RE ALL SNAKEBIT: ANTIDOTE INSIDE

## Michael A. Jones

NEW PARADIGM MEDIA
GRESHAM, OREGON

Edited by Ken McFarland
Page composition by Page One Communications
Cover design by Frank DeSantis

ISBN: 978-0-578-13103-0

# Contents

# Dedication

I am dedicating this book to every individual who suffers from some form of mental unwellness.

Whether you suffer from depression, anxiety disorder, a sick fantasy life, hear voices, or just don't think straight, I believe a daily processing of the principles in this book will help you get better and avoid making bad decisions.

I also dedicate this book to you who are addicted to success, power, money, substances, food, or something else. I am very hopeful that you will find freedom here from whatever counterfeit god may have you in its power.

—Mike Jones

# My Rationale for This Book

## We're All Snakebit: Here's the Solution You Might Not Be Expecting

**M**y objective is to write a book that demonstrates we're all snakebit and that sooner or later all of us will make some terribly wrong decisions when dealing with life's challenges. I will contend that the solution to our issues isn't to become a smarter person but rather to become a different person.

Becoming a different person is radical stuff. If you're just looking to smooth off a few rough edges from your personality, this book's not for you. In fact, you'll do better with this book if you're a bit desperate, perhaps out of control in some area of your life—or if you know someone who is and might share this book with them.

Unlike mainstream psychotherapy, which emphasizes becoming better at handling your issues through enhanced self-understanding (maybe with the help of a therapist), I will operate from the biblical premise that self is actually our main problem. By self, I'm talking about you and me at our core. My contention? We're all too sick to get well (think *proud, selfish, lazy, deceitful, rigid, out of control—don't need any outside help, thank you*).

Psychiatrist M. Scott Peck says we're all snakebit (*mentally ill* is his term), just to different degrees.

This book will posit that the only solution to our issues is for us to get replaced—every day.

My own personal snakebitness centered on an addiction that began in my teen years and dominated my life for nearly forty years. I fell into the grip of a terribly ill fantasy life that took me down at will. I became mentally ill worshiping this counterfeit god that was slowly killing me on the inside.

Then fifteen years ago I unexpectedly discovered the amazing solution to my unwellness.

I didn't get better—I got replaced. I became a different person. And I got well.

You can read the rest of the story in these pages. And my hope is that you'll find some answers that will enable you to overcome your own snakebitness in whatever form it takes.

I submit the following Bible texts as a further illustration of the universal problem we all have to deal with when it comes to who we are by nature.

*"The heart is deceitful above all things, and desperately corrupt... incurable...who can understand it!" "The whole head is sick..."* (Jeremiah 17:9; Isaiah 1:5).

I offer the following Scriptures as pointing to the solution and what it looks like.

*"Put off your old self which is being corrupted by its evil desires... and put on the new self created to be like God." "The Holy Spirit will come upon you in power...and you will be changed into a different person"* (Ephesians 4:22-24; 1 Samuel 10:6).

Throughout this book, I will attempt to describe a process that will help you become *warm, patient, loving, selfless, gracious, without guile—a real sweetheart.*

You may think you're this way already. But let me ask you, how do you react when someone wreaks physical or emotional havoc on you or one of your family members?

Anyway, I must tell you, most folks don't get this. It's the Holy Spirit's work to help you get it. And if you're willing, He will help you find what the writer of the following poem couldn't   a satisfying, fulfilling new life of patience, peace, love and joy, no matter how badly your life may be going just now.

# "Something More!"

He'd walked all the roads there were to walk
and some there never was.
He'd asked two and twenty questions
never learning the because.
And he knew that his life would not be
what it was before.
Still he knew there must be something more.

He'd seen all the towns there were to see
in countries old and new.
He'd done half the things that young men
half his age were wont to do.
He'd walked meadow, hill, and highway
knocking once on every door.
Always looking, seeking, needing something more.

As a young man he grew skyward
and tall as any tree,
He was strong of muscle, wide of will

*as young men ought to be.*
*His young eyes had left the apple*
*fastened to the core.*
*For he knew that there must be something more.*

*Still firm of frame though forty*
*he awoke one day to find*
*that the crimson flower of madness*
*had blossomed on his mind,*
*and the wind of constant wanting*
*had in secret won the war.*
*Still he prayed that there might be something more.*

*And the fine sun of fifty*
*saw him dying and alone.*
*Just a man struck down suddenly*
*by something not yet known.*
*Just a man who spent all his life*
*hoping once to soar.*
*And all the while expecting something more.*

*Are we all then like that young man*
*who wanted so to fly?*
*Who gave his life pursuing life*
*and daring to ask why.*
*Daring death to walk beyond the ground*
*that had been walked before.*
*Expecting to be offered something more.*

*God, but there must be something more.*

—Rod McKuen

# CHAPTER ONE

# We're All Snakebit

## Human nature can't be fixed

I was about 9 or 10 when the snake bit me.

It happened so fast I can still hardly believe it. As a young boy, I grew up in the country in a home outside Grand Rapids, Michigan. Not having siblings, I became intimately acquainted with nature. I used to feed crickets or grasshoppers to praying mantises and had many an ant fight atop the cement well cover behind our house. In winter I'd often take apples to the rabbits in the woods behind our house when the snow got deep.

One balmy summer day I caught a small garter snake and began playing with it in our dirt driveway. I called him Snakie, and we played a game of catch and release. That meant I'd carry Snakie into the driveway, and he'd try to get away to the safety of the long grass in the adjacent field. Just before he'd make it, I'd catch him and bring him back to the driveway—over and over again.

In time, my mother noticed what was going on and warned me, *"Mikie, you'd better stop playing with that snake or you're going to get bit."*

*"Aw, c'mon, Mom,"* I replied. *"He's my friend. He likes me."* With a final warning that Snakie might not really be my friend, Mom went back into the house—and Snakie and I continued to play our game. Time and again, Snakie would almost slither to the safety of the field, when I would catch him and bring him back to the driveway, where I could continue playing with him.

Finally after about the tenth time that he tried to get away only to have me catch him, Snakie had enough.

What happened next happened in a flash. Snakie struck. He bit me on a finger. In a moment of sheer terror, I leaped to my feet, shook him off, and raced into the house, my finger dripping with blood.

I was snakebit.

Of course, you already know this little garter snake wasn't venomous. But I was terrified and don't recall ever playing with snakes again, though I'm sorry to say I killed a few. One was a poisonous copperhead that my 11-year-old son, Mikie, captured by the Shenandoah River and brought up to the house, totally oblivious to the fact that his life was in danger.

You don't have to play with snakes to be snakebit. Your birth guarantees that condition. Fact is, since Eve listened to a talking snake, we've all emerged from our mothers' wombs snakebit in some way—self-centered, anxious or depressed, deceitful, overly sensitive, addictive, unwell physically or mentally, rebellious, some of us even prone to violence. And none of us thinks straight.

## Human Nature Is Ruined

The old Merle Haggard song, *"Ramblin' Fever,"* gets it right with the lyric, *"There ain't no kind of cure for my disease."* We are who we are— sick to death at our core.

Some of us modify our behavior, but few of us ever change basically. People who like to fight are usually ready to do battle. Anxious, fearful people tend to stay that way. Addicts tend to retain their addictions.

Another problem associated with being snakebit is this: Most of us think we're all right when we're not. It's really hard to help people like us.

Back to my contention that we're all snakebit—the news on your iPhone app or on your evening television news should make my point. Whether it's a prominent public official's immorality or someone else getting busted for abusing, stealing, or killing someone, the news overwhelmingly reminds us: *Human nature is ruined and can't be fixed.*

And the idea that I'm not so bad—that I just need to develop my good side—is an oxymoron. No one has a good side. Think about it. Who among us hasn't at some time had the urge to kill or indulge some other corrupt thought even though we didn't act on it? Our occasional moments of altruism come from the grace of God to which we sometimes respond.

When it comes to the human condition, King David, of the Bible, wrote, *"Surely I was [snakebit] at birth, [snakebit] from the time my mother conceived me"* (Psalm 51:5).[1]

Now David was a good guy who did the right thing most of the time. Until, of course, he had an affair with a married woman and had her husband killed trying to cover up what he had done. Even good guys are snakebit. Remember Bill Clinton, Lance Armstrong, Tiger Woods, Alex Rodriguez, and whoever else of prominence may have fallen recently. Then, of course, there's you and me.

Who among us hasn't at some time said or done something about which we later said, *"I can't believe I said that—or did that"*? Those are the moments that remind us—we're all snakebit.

I still remember telling my first lie. It took place in a church, of all places. Two of the kids in our neighborhood—a brother and sister—had invited me to attend some meetings at their church. I was around 9 years of age and had recently strummed on a guitar at my Aunt Goldy's house. So when an announcement was made for kids who could play a musical instrument to make themselves known, my neighborhood friends asked me if I could play an instrument.

*"A guitar or violin?"* I replied, trying to appear cool. *"Go and sign up,"* they said, almost pushing me into the aisle to join the other kids who really did know how to play an instrument. Unbelievably, I got up and kept going. Inexplicably, when asked what instrument I'd be playing, I said, *"A violin or guitar, I'm not sure which."* Later, horrified, I confessed to my mother and said I didn't want to go back.

*"Oh, you're going back,"* she replied. *"And you're going to tell that minister that you lied and that you don't know how to play any musical instrument."*

*"Please don't make me go back,"* I pleaded. But Mother was unrelenting. I was going to have to face the music. I had lied. Knowing I had to own up kept me in agony for a week.

---

1.     David used the term *sinful* in the original Hebrew, not *snakebit*.

Finally the terrible day arrived. Once I got to the church, I found the minister and confessed that I didn't know how to play any musical instrument, that I was sorry I hadn't told the truth, and would he please remove my name from his recital list. He was gracious and said he would take care of the matter. I was so relieved I almost jumped for joy.

But something awful was about to happen. The minister forgot to remove my name from his list.

Picture me sitting with my friends rejoicing that the matter was resolved. Then you won't find it hard to imagine my shock when midway through the recital, the minister announced, *"Now we'll have a violin or guitar solo from Mikie Jones."*

With tears streaming down my face, I stood up and said, *"But I told you, Reverend Tompkins, that I don't know how to play a guitar or a violin,"* as I made my way to him, sobbing. *"There, there,"* he said, as he put his arm around me and announced the next kid who really did know how to play a musical instrument, *"It's all right, it's okay."*

But it wasn't okay. And I've never forgotten that terrible moment. A lot of years have passed, and I still can't fathom why in the world I told that lie except for one reason. I was snakebit.

You're snakebit, too. You may not tell fibs. But you may have an inferiority complex, suffer from fear or anxiety, have a short fuse, get dragged down by depression, or be addicted to something (food, a substance, alcohol, your job, a relationship?). Ever cheat on someone or fudge on your taxes? Are you sick much of the time?

You could even be snakebit by your success. Like maybe you're a CEO, professional athlete, or a TV anchor whose life is consumed by your job—and your family barely knows you. Very few maintain balance in the face of significant success. *Let's face it, in some way we're all snakebit.*

In the next chapter I will share with you the secret that transformed my life about fifteen years ago from the snakebite of a devastating addiction.

# Chapter Two

# Becoming the Person You Were Meant to Be

I was watching a nature program on TV recently and viewed the story of a man who raised poisonous snakes and had been bitten by one. He lived alone but was able to call 911. However, by the time the ambulance picked him up, he had lost his ability to speak.

When the ambulance medics, and later, the medical personnel at the nearby hospital asked him what kind of snake had bitten him, his vocal cords paralyzed, he wasn't able to reply. To save his life, the doctors needed to know what kind of antivenom he needed. Time was of the essence because his body was shutting down. Finally a friend raced to his house, found the snake which was still loose, and called the hospital with the snake's identity. The man's life was saved.

I contended in the first chapter that we're all snakebit. Indeed, our entire planet is snakebit. Which is why nothing works right and everything dies sooner or later including you and me.

As I write this, even though we were designed to live forever, an estimated 153,000 of us die every day worldwide. In terms of nothing working correctly, I still recall when an Air France airbus crashed a few years ago when the plane's instruments malfunctioned, and 228 people died in a snakebit airplane. But all this death likely won't hit home until someone dies in front of you—or until you're faced with just one death.

On that point, I still remember Lester, the white-haired 68-year-old with congestive heart failure who motioned me to his hospital bedside when I was a young pastor. As I bent to listen, I was shocked and didn't immediately know how to respond when he whispered hoarsely, *"Mike, would you do my funeral after I'm gone?"*

And then there was the 17-year-old boy who drowned in a bathtub following a seizure just a year ago when I was a relief chaplain at a local hospital. I arrived at the hospital ER at the same time his horrified parents got there. I mean, what do you say? *"Sorry, you lost your kid!"* I didn't say much. Just cried and prayed with them, then went home and didn't sleep the rest of the night. As you can imagine, the entire experience was a nightmare.

Whether it's a bad heart, a defeated kidney, mental unwellness, or a nasty disposition, we're all snakebit in some way. The Bible explains that when the first man and woman sold out to a snake, they lost their ability to be kind and loving. Instead they became deceitful and unloving. Our popular music often touches on such matters. Remember the Taylor Swift song, *"Why do you have to be so mean?"* Or Mick Jagger's lyrical lament, *"Can't get no satisfaction."*

Speaking of satisfaction, I found fascinating the commentary by *Washington Post* columnist Kathleen Parker on women. Women are achieving more parity in the workforce than ever before, she writes. *"But guess what? They're still not happy."*

She points out that *"the things that matter most—equilibrium, inner peace, wisdom, heart, and a family that isn't in constant chaos"* are intangibles largely ignored by women on the climb. I will contend throughout this book that to become the person you were meant to be will not be based on workplace success but will depend most on a lifeswap. WE'RE ALL SNAKEBIT, women and men alike, and need a heart transplant so we can obtain a new core.

Whether we're successful in business or elsewhere, the fact remains, we're all snakebit—addictive, vindictive, unbalanced in some way. I mean when you think about it, don't certain characteristics in your life come to mind that you wish were different? You may suffer from depression, anxiety, or fibromyalgia—you may be negative and critical, or your body lets you down. There are lots of ways to be snakebit.

As you must know, even the brightest and the best are snakebit in some way. Consider the late billionaire Steve Jobs of Apple. He died early at age 56 because he refused his doctor's advice for his quite-curable cancer until it was too late. Like that old Frank Sinatra song, he did things his way, and it killed him. He was brilliant but snakebit. Being snakebit always trumps intellect.

I used to do things my way. But my life changed dramatically after I became a Christian at age 30. I still remember telling the married woman with whom I was having an affair about my commitment to Christ. Her response was, *"You're never going to touch me again, are you?"* And I said, *"No, I love you too much now."*

I wasn't just being glib. The reality of this immoral relationship was that we were simply using each other to meet needs. With Christ in my life, I began to let my Creator start meeting my deeper needs. However, the person I'd been seeing went on to have another affair and broke up two homes—hers and the guy's she was seeing. They married, had a glamorous honeymoon on a tropical island, and were divorced in about a year. She never married again.

As for me, my life was improving, though I had yet to learn about the Exchanged Life (see chapter 4) and the transformation it would bring to me. Even so, I stopped cheating, and my first marriage went on for another fourteen years. I also stopped smoking cigarettes.

But about fifteen years ago, I had an epiphany that launched me out of my snakebit existence into a totally different life from anything I had known before. It also freed me from my devastating forty-year addiction. *Bottom line: I exchanged my original life for a new one—literally! I didn't learn how to become a better person—I learned how to become a different person.*

Prior to this, I still had significant issues. I had issues with fear, an inordinate love need, sexual addiction issues, a terribly unwell fantasy life, and a growing addiction to alcohol—fine wines being my drug of choice. But fifteen years ago I began to realize that traditional Christianity (making a public decision for Jesus Christ and attending church most every week) wasn't working for me when it came to transformation. So I tried something else.

*I finally accepted that my snakebit human nature was ruined and couldn't be fixed—couldn't be healed. It could only be replaced. It's the purpose of this book to show you how to do this.*

P.S. The process for doing this is not one and done. For a successful outcome, you'll need to enter a spiritual chrysalis every day. That's where the transformation takes place that leads to the emergence of a new you. But, hey, read the "Heart of the Matter" chapter first. Then you'll understand more fully what I'm trying to say.

# CHAPTER THREE

# Heart of the Matter

In recent years, a fascinating phenomenon has been taking place with heart-transplant patients. What's so intriguing is that an increasing number of these patients believe they are taking on some of the characteristics of their donors.

What does this have to do with you? Quite a lot actually because I'm recommending that you get a similar kind of surgery. But first, consider these anecdotes to help you understand why I'm suggesting you get your own spiritual heart transplant.

Bill Sheridan had drawing skills that you might expect of a child. But as he convalesced after a heart-transplant operation, he was suddenly blessed with an artistic talent he hadn't had before that enabled him to go from drawing stick figures to producing beautiful drawings of wildlife and landscapes.

When Sheridan was able to meet the mother of the donor, a 24-year-old stockbroker, he asked her if her son had been artistic. She told him her son had loved to paint and had shown an artistic bent when he was only 18 months old.

Bill Wohl, another heart transplant patient, was a Type A, 58-year-old, money-obsessed businessman until his transplant five years ago. Today he works part time and spends most of his newfound energy winning speed and performance medals in swimming, cycling, and track. It's a passion matched only by the good he wants to do with his new charitable foundation.

And there's one other thing: He surprises himself by tearing up whenever he hears music by a singer called Slade—a reaction unimaginable before his transplant.

Months later Wohl was given the opportunity to contact the family of the donor. That was when he learned he had the heart of a 36-year-old Hollywood stunt man who had loved Slade's music.

He was stunned.

Claire Sylvia, a 47-year-old dancer and divorced mother of one, was dying of pulmonary hypertension when she received a heart-lung transplant with organs from an 18-year-old boy who had been killed in a motorcycle accident.

In a book she wrote later entitled *Change of Heart,* she was asked a few weeks after the surgery by a reporter, *"Now that you've had this miracle, what do you want more than anything else?"* She replied, *"Actually, I'm dying for a beer right now."*

She said she was mortified by her flippant answer. *"I didn't even like beer,"* she said. *"But the craving I felt at that moment was specifically for the taste of beer."*

As she monitored other changes she was beginning to experience, she found herself having acquired a bizarre fondness for certain foods she had never liked before: Snickers bars, green peppers, and Kentucky Fried Chicken were among them, and she began to wonder if her new heart had its own set of tastes and preferences.

It seemed that it did. Months later she was able to meet the donor's family and learned that the young man whose heart she had received drank beer and loved the foods that she now loved. In fact, he had died with an order of Chicken McNuggets beneath his jacket when his motorcycle crashed into a tree.

Similar anecdotes abound from other transplant patients. However, most of their physicians pooh-pooh the idea that the heart is anything more than a pump and certainly not capable of transferring donor characteristics. Tucson cardiologist Jack Copeland is an exception. He notes, *"With any solid organ, you are transferring DNA from the donor to the recipient. So there may be something to this..."*

What do you think? Does it seem plausible to you that heart-transplant patients can receive characteristics from their donors' organs even though they have no idea who these people were? And what about the spiritual hearts people receive when they open their lives to God and exchange their original self for a new one?

If you're like me, you'll be fascinated with some new information about the heart that comes from the doctoral research of Dr. Linda Caviness, a professor of education at La Sierra University. She told me that for years many Bible scholars believed that the Bible text that says, *"As a man thinketh in his heart, so is he"* (Proverbs 23:7) was talking about the mind and the brain.

However, Dr. Caviness' learned during her doctoral research that the heart is a sensory organ with a small brain of its own and that it has an ability to actually influence the brain. Only recently, she says, have neurocardiologists discovered neurons in the heart—about 40,000 on average, providing strong evidence that the heart may have its own brain and memory system.

She says there are more connections going from the heart to the brain than from the brain to the heart. And she reports that the electrical current of the heart is forty to sixty times stronger than the electrical current of the brain.

You know how you're repelled by some people and drawn to others and don't always know why? Might it be the state of a person's heart that draws or repels? What do you think? Dr. Caviness' research shows that the heart has an electrical-magnetic field that can be measured up to five feet out from the body, whereas the brain's electrical-magnetic field only measures out two inches.

What kind of influence emanates from your heart's magnetic field?

I should probably confess here that for much of my life I tried to be a Christian while I had the heart of the devil! Let me explain. If you're familiar with the Bible, you know the Jewish religious leaders didn't like Jesus any too well when He told them their father was the devil? They had just claimed that God was their father, but Jesus told them, *"You belong to your father the devil..."* (John 8:44).

Jesus wasn't slamming them. He was simply alluding to the fact that each one of us has the devil for a spiritual father unless we've had a spiritual heart transplant. The apostle Paul says we need such a transplant every day. *"I die daily,"* he wrote to the church in Corinth, Greece. *"I really mean that"* (1 Corinthians 15:31).

All of us trace our parentage to Adam and Eve. But keep in mind, once they fell, they took on Satan's DNA, and he became their spiritual father. Each of us has been infected from birth ever since.

The Bible is clear that our human nature is fatally flawed, ruined, can't be fixed. And the idea of working on my good self is simply irrational. There is no such thing as a good self, according to the Scriptures. Why spend time working on that which can't be fixed?

When I was baptized in Grand Rapids, Michigan, at the age of 11, I received a heart transplant. But I didn't know that I needed to get a new one every day. Perhaps the pastor guiding me didn't think I'd understand. Anyway, it didn't take very long for my new heart to be rejected by the antibodies of my natural self.

As a teenager, my religious life became a holy bore as the devil stung me with a sin of addiction. It was a sin that slowly leeched God's life out of me as my new heart became stony. Indeed, for most of the next forty-plus years I waged a losing battle against this addiction despite a Christian commitment.

Even after I made an adult decision for Christ at the age of 30, I still struggled. I prayed about the problem, got many a victory, only to suffer many a defeat. It was a teeter-totter experience. *Why so much defeat?* I was trying to live a high-integrity life out of a self life that was demonic at its core. I needed to have what this book will refer to as the Exchanged Life. But I didn't understand that. I really didn't have a chance.

With respect to our addictions, I would point out that some of them can generate a high that can take your breath away. I have come to believe that this kind of high is often demonically enhanced.

One thing is for sure. The high from our addictions is always fleeting and always gives way to depression. Why depression? Because doing the wrong thing always deadens and destroys us. Even while we're enjoying the high, depression is licking its chops, waiting to do its devastating work.

About fifteen years ago, I asked God to kill my addiction. And if he couldn't give me a complete victory, I told Him, then He could kill me literally. *"Just take me out,"* I told Him. It was a ferocious struggle as I wrestled with God for a victory over addictive thoughts and behavior (my counterfeit gods) that were dominating my life.

Emotionally I felt as if I'd rather die than give up my addiction. As I just mentioned, I had even begun acting out when I was single after many years of struggling with an illicit thought life.

So I made the decision to die to my ruined self. In the process, when God answered, He did two amazing things: (1) He replaced me, and (2) He destroyed the monster (the false god) that had me. In the process, He also changed me into a different person, a wonderful gift He renews for me every day even now, these many years later.

Perhaps you struggle with your own snakebit self. The manifestations could be your critical spirit, hot temper, fear, alcohol addiction, use of illicit drugs, depression, insecurity, homosexuality, porn, overeating, snakebit thinking, or something else that takes you down. *Whatever it is, know that a daily spiritual heart transplant—a metamorphosis into a different person—will be your ultimate solution.*

Let me make it clear, this is an exchange of one nature for another, the human/demonic for the human/divine. Want to check it out?

If you do, it's important for you to understand that your natural self won't go easily. It seethes with hostility toward that which is spiritual and is always trying for a comeback. In fact, the rebellious self we're all born with reminds me of the robot from the future in that old Terminator 2 movie from the early 1990s with Arnold Schwarzenegger and Linda Hamilton.

In the movie, Linda and her son are chased relentlessly by a robot who's been sent back in time to kill her son, who will one day save the human race. Schwarzenegger also plays a robot from the future. His job is to safeguard her son.

During the chases that ensue, Arnold and Linda blast the bad robot (think demonic self) full of holes and sometimes into pieces. But the robot seems to be indestructible. His pieces always come back together, and he resumes the chase throughout the movie until he's finally destroyed, interestingly, in a lake of fire.

It seems to me that the natural self is much like this. We hardly seem to get a victory over our former self when to our dismay it shows up again. Even after Jesus has blasted it into submission when we've sought His help, and just when we think it's finally gone, self rears its ugly head. It seems like a never-ending battle—and it is.

Just know that when you exchange your old life for a new one every morning and you ingest enough of God's grace, you'll find yourself starting to live a life of victory over your old snakebit self. Jesus made it clear that this exchange must be daily: *"If anyone would follow Me, let him deny himself and take up his cross **daily** and follow Me"* (Luke 9:23).

I will attempt to provide a protocol in the next chapter that will enable you to transition from an ugly caterpillar self to a beautiful butterfly self every day. Why must I reprocess this every day, you may ask? All I can tell you is what the Bible states:

*"The old [snakebit] nature loves to do evil...and the Holy Spirit gives us desires that are opposite from what the evil [snakebit] nature desires. These two forces are constantly fighting each other, and your choices are never free from this conflict"* (Galatians 5:17-18).

Your old caterpillar self is always trying to replace your butterfly self.

You say you're pretty weak? Actually that's good news because God says:

*"My grace is sufficient for you, for my power is made perfect in weakness"* (2 Corinthians 12:9).

What you'll love about this very different life is its fruitage. Once you have it, you simply go from being a snakebit, self-centered so-and-so to becoming a winsome person with a divine DNA. You will start living a life of purity, peace, joy, love, and self control. Self control is one of the greater gifts.

Follow the protocol in the next chapter, and every day the Holy Spirit will remove your old self and reinstall the heavenly software of a new self *"created to be like God"* (Ephesians 4:24). The fruitage of the new self is *"love, joy, peace, patience, kindness"* and an awesome list of additional attributes you'll be thrilled to have.

Next I'll describe in greater detail the process through which you can obtain this experience. And as you exchange your present life for this new one, I promise you, you're going to love your new life. For starters, claim God's promise to *"give you a new heart, and put within you a right Spirit, and take away your heart of stone, and give you a heart of flesh"* (Ezekiel 36:26).

All you need to do is ask. The Spirit of the Creator-God is longing to hear from you and to make this request your reality. The Bible tells us in James 4:5, *"The Spirit whom He has caused to live within us longs for us with a jealous love."* More about this in the next few chapters.

# CHAPTER FOUR

# Dying to Live!

The protocol which follows is based on my belief in the Creator-God of the Bible. Now, you may not believe as I do. Your belief might be based on a higher power, but you're not sure about who or what it is. Or you may not believe in much of anything.

Just know this: You don't need to be in lockstep with me in order for these points to help you. You need only to accept that you're snakebit and be willing to experiment that the Creator-God might be working in your life. After all, He does invite you to experiment—to *"taste and see that the Lord is good"* (Psalm 34:8).

But first, let me reiterate that the Creator-God's purpose for our lives is that we should become beautiful people—*kind, unselfish, patient, gracious, loving. Real sweethearts.* Not quick to take offense. Easy to be with—beautiful on the inside no matter what we look like on the outside.

To give you a clearer expectation of what God has in mind for you, I want to share with you the metamorphosis through which caterpillars become butterflies. But first, let's look at the dictionary definition of the word *metamorphosis*.[1]

**Metamorphosis:** *A complete change of form, structure, or substance. The process of transformation from an immature form to an adult form*

---

1.  Definitions are from *The Random House College Dictionary*, revised.

*in two or more distinct stages. A change in the nature of a person into a completely different one. A marked change in appearance, character, condition, or appearance.*

With these definitions in mind, let's examine how a caterpillar becomes a butterfly. During its first two weeks of life, the caterpillar eats 3,000 times its original weight, then spins a chrysalis and dies. On Day 1 the caterpillar's digestive tract starts to go, and a fascinating process continues for the next ten days that results in the total death of the caterpillar and birth of a butterfly.

Those who study butterflies report that there's no butterfly lurking in the caterpillar waiting to get out. In fact, the butterfly gets created from scratch during the ten-day period after the caterpillar disappears into the chrysalis. Incredibly, MRIs show that the butterfly's organs are nonexistent in the caterpillar.

This makes it all the more amazing that when the butterfly emerges from the chrysalis. It is a totally different creature from the one that launched the process. For instance, the caterpillar's eye is simple and can only see light. But the butterfly's eye is complex and can see color and for long distances.

The caterpillar can only crawl, whereas the butterfly can fly. Its four wings have thousands of microscopic scales much like the tiles on the space shuttle, and one butterfly—the Monarch—can fly for thousands of miles from Canada to Mexico and back.

Scientists who study butterflies say that the metamorphosis from caterpillar to butterfly is one of the great wonders of the natural world.

I would submit to you that the metamorphosis from caterpillar person to a butterfly being is an even greater wonder. Perhaps that is why the Bible tells us, *"If anyone is in Christ, he is a new creation. The old has gone, the new has come"* (2 Corinthians 5:17).

I suspect the reverse was true for Jesus Christ in coming here. From eternity Jesus is a spectacular Being whom the Bible identifies as Creator.[2] But the Scriptures say He *"would make Himself nothing"* so He could do His chrysalis time for nine months in the womb of a Jewish peasant girl and become one of us (more about that on p. 149).

---

2. *"He created everything there is. Nothing exists that He didn't make"* (John 1:3).

By the way, since His followers are promised a new body one day that will be just like His,[3] you might find interesting what Jesus' glorified body looks like. Here's a description recorded by His last surviving disciple, John, after Jesus paid him a visit when he was old, likely in his 90s:

*"His head and His hair were white like wool, as white as snow. And His eyes were bright like flames of fire. His feet were as bright as bronze refined in a furnace, and His voice thundered like mighty ocean waves.... And His face was as bright as the sun in all its brilliance"* (Revelation 1:14, 16).

The Bible tells us elsewhere that Jesus is big enough *"to fill the whole universe"* but that He can make Himself small enough *"to live in your heart"* (Ephesians 4:10 and 3:17). I share this information so you can have confidence that He can change you into a beautiful person who's no longer snakebit but at peace with yourself and coping successfully with life's issues.

Your biggest issue is likely to be your ego and admitting that you really can't fix yourself. Just know that you're safe with this power.

After all, this is your Creator, and He died for you. So *experiment with the steps that follow, and He will change you into an exciting new you!*[4] The "old you" can't be fixed, can't be spruced up, cleaned up, or restored. The old you has to go. You have to be willing to let it go totally. Speaking to that point, the apostle Paul once wrote, *"I die daily. I really mean that"* (1 Corinthians 15:31).

Imagine that you have an old beater of a car (no big stretch for some of us!). It's rusty, the engine clanks and sputters, it burns so much oil that you leave a trail of smoke everywhere you go, and the upholstery inside is riddled with holes and cracks. But a wealthy friend of yours offers to swap it out—no cash required—for a brand-new gleaming Lexus (or Mercedes or Cadillac or BMW—any luxury car of your choice). All you have to do is trade in your old clunker and let your friend scrap it. Would this kind of exchange interest you?

Well, this is very much like the kind of exchange God offers you: your old life—the old you—for an all-new one: your old snakebit nature for a

---

3.   *"Our heavenly bodies will be just like Christ's"* (1 Corinthians 15:48, NLT).

4.   *"If anyone is in Christ, he is a new creation"* (2 Corinthians 5:17).

new nature, your old heart for a new one, your old mind for the mind of Jesus. I like to call this *The Exchanged Life*. It's as real as your next breath, and it's available to you any time you're ready.

So exactly HOW can you go about receiving an Exchanged Life? It's not complicated. Just follow this simple, step-by-step *"Become-a-New-You"* protocol. You'll likely create your own one of these days. For now, I'm suggesting you use this one to get started.

## The Become-a-New-You Protocol

Think about what follows as akin to a caterpillar going into a chrysalis, dying, and emerging as a beautiful butterfly. These points are intended to get you into and through your own spiritual metamorphosis *every day* so that the Holy Spirit can enable you to die to self and emerge transformed into a new you. Because your former caterpillar self is always trying for a comeback, relentlessly follow the protocol noted here and ingest the Scriptures in the next section daily for a successful outcome.

1. **Invite God into your life every morning before you do anything else.** Jesus says, *"I stand at the door and knock. If anyone opens the door, I will come in"* (Revelation 3:20). So tell Him, *"Lord, please come in. I choose to give You unrestricted access into my life and to surrender my will to Your will."*

2. **Ask God to give you a new or renewed heart and to install His mind in place of yours.** Just say, *"Lord, You've promised to give me a new heart and said I can have 'the mind of Christ.' Please give me these two gifts today through your indwelling Holy Spirit"* (Ezekiel 36:26; 1 Corinthians 2:16).

3. **Also ask God to change you into a new person via Ephesians 4:22-24 and 1 Samuel 10:6:** *"Put off your old self which is being corrupted by its evil desires...and put on the new self created to be like God."* And *"The Spirit of the Lord will come upon you with power...and you will be changed into a different person."* Please make these words efficacious in my life right now, I pray in Jesus' name.

4. **Next, go to the cross (in your mind's eye) and look to Jesus.** When the Israelites of old rebelled and found themselves being

bitten by deadly sand vipers and were dying (Numbers 21), God told them to look at an artificial snake hanging on a pole. This didn't make any sense, but it worked. Those who looked lived, and those who didn't died. The bronze snake was a symbol of a Savior to come, *who says to you today, "Hey, you're snakebit, too. Look to Me and be saved"* (Isaiah 45:22). So spend a few minutes at the Cross! Jesus spent six hours there bleeding out for you. *Got just one drop of faith? Use it! Look and live!* This is one of the few places where it's okay to say, *"Oh, my God!"* before you leave.

5. **Ask God to infuse His grace into your life.** He tells us in Scripture, *"My grace is sufficient for you, for My power is made perfect in weakness"* (2 Corinthians 12:9). God's grace is a mysterious attribute of the Godhead which is lethal to your old nature and brings divine life to your new self. (For more about grace, go to p. 163.)

6. **Tell God out loud, *"Thank You for transforming me into a different person.*** Do you suffer from low self esteem? It's time to start getting over that. *"Those who are led by the Spirit of God are sons [and daughters] of God . . . heirs of God and co-heirs with Christ"* (Romans 8:14, 17). Jesus has promised that one day you—yes, you—will sit with Him on His throne (Revelation 3:21) assisting in the administration of the universe.[5]

7. **Practice "eating" God's Bible promises.** The prophet Jeremiah once wrote, *"When Your words came, I ate them. They were my joy and my heart's delight."*—Jeremiah 15:16. Here's an example of how you can *eat* one of God's promises: Just say, *"Lord, the Bible says You've given (me) your very great and precious promises so that through them (I) might participate in (Your) divine nature and escape the corruption in the world caused by evil desires* (see 2 Peter 1:4). Please make this promise a reality in my life right now by pouring Your love into my new heart, I ask in Jesus' name."

*Now reflect on your new identity in Jesus Christ. **You're royalty now!*** Let that fact sink in. Over time, that truth will enhance your new godly self esteem and help you maintain the new you! You're an ambassador-in-training of the King of the universe—a universe believed (at this writing)

---

5.  God says He will put His faithful servant "in charge of all His possessions" (Matthew 24:47).

to include 500 billion galaxies! Expect intergalactic space travel, likely at the speed of thought, to be in your future as you speed through the universe on missions for God throughout the ceaseless ages of eternity. Did you think you were just going to hang out on a cloud once you got to heaven?

Now begin ingesting the promises on the next few pages and in *"Praying Yourself to Death"* on p. 159 to continue your metamorphosis into an amazing new person who's exchanged his/her old life for a new one. You're on your way to awesome, my friend!

## Some Scriptures to Ingest As You Continue Your Spiritual Metamorphosis

When He had seventy disciples, Jesus told them, *"Whoever eats My flesh and drinks My blood has eternal life."* And fifty-eight left Him. To the twelve who were left, He explained: *"The flesh counts for nothing. The words I have spoken to you are spirit and they are life"* (John 6:54, 63). The prophet Jeremiah once wrote, *"When Your words came, I ate them"* (Jeremiah 15:16). Try "eating" the promises which follow every day by claiming them and asking the Holy Spirit to implant them in your being. The result will be an amazing new you—new and renewed daily.

## Sample Prayer and Protocol

Good morning, Father. It's your (son or daughter)_____, down here in the war zone of Earth and coming in the name of Jesus Christ before Your throne of grace to continue my metamorphosis into a new me. Lord, You've said in Scripture, *"I stand at the door and knock. If anyone opens the door, I'll come in and we'll share a meal as friends"* (Revelation 3:20). Please come in.

You've also said, *"Fear not, for I am with you; be not dismayed, for I am your God. I will help you, I will strengthen you, I will uphold you with My victorious right hand"* (Isaiah 41:10). I claim this promise for myself right now in Jesus' name so I can get through today's challenges successfully.

Lord, You've also told me, *"Fear not, for I have redeemed you, I have called you by name* [your name here]; *you are Mine. When you pass through the waters, I will be with you; and through the rivers, they will not* [drown] *you. When you walk through the fire, you will not be burned, neither will the flame kindle upon you, for I am the Lord Your God, the Holy One of Israel, your Savior...and I love you"* (Isaiah 43:1-3, 5). I claim this promise also.

Please go before me today, Father. You've said in Scripture:

*"It is the Lord who goes before you; He will not fail you nor forsake you; do not fear or be dismayed"* (Deuteronomy 31:8).

Lord, thank You for this amazing promise:

*"The Lord says, 'I will rescue those who love Me, I will protect those who trust in My Name; when they call upon Me, I will answer. I'll be with them in trouble, I will rescue them and honor them, I will satisfy them with a long life and give them my salvation'"* (Psalm 91:14-16).

## Claim These Four Exchanged-Life Promises

Lord, You've also promised, *"We have the mind of Christ." "Don't copy the behavior and customs of this world, but let God transform you into a new person **by changing the way you think**"* (1 Corinthians 2:16; Romans 12:2). I invite You to install within me the mind of Christ and remove my mind so I can think correctly.

*"The Spirit of the Lord will come upon you with power...and you will be changed into a different person"* (1 Samuel 10:6). The door is open, dear Holy Spirit. Please change me today into a new person who is like You in character and conduct.

*"I've been crucified with Christ; **it is no longer I who live, but Christ Who lives in me**. And the life I now live in the flesh, I live by faith in the Son of God Who loved me and gave Himself for me"* (Galatians 2:20). May these words become my reality today, I ask in Jesus' name.

*"If anyone is in Christ, he is a new creation; the old has gone, the new has come"* (2 Corinthians 5:17).

## Claim These Promises Also

*"I will never leave you nor forsake you"* (Hebrews 13:5).[6]

Father, You've said, *"For our sake You made [Jesus] to be sin who knew no sin that in Him I might become the righteousness of God"* (2 Corinthians 5:21). I choose to place my life within Jesus' life right now as the Holy Spirit makes my choice a reality.

I choose to be emptied of self now, Lord, so I can be filled with You and Your love. You've promised, *"And to know the love of Christ, which surpasses knowledge that [I] may be filled with all the fullness of God"* (Ephesians 3:19). Please fill me now with all of the fullness of the Godhead, I pray, and continue to pour Your love into my heart (Romans 5:5).

Lord, You've said, *"Don't get drunk.... Instead be filled with the Holy Spirit"* (Ephesians 5:18). Please fill me with the Holy Spirit right now, I pray, as I turn away from alcohol and drugs.

Jesus, You've also said, *"Behold, I give you power...over all the power of the enemy" "Nothing will be impossible to you"* (Luke 10:19; Matthew 17:20). May these promises become my reality, I pray.

And Lord, You've promised, *"I will dwell in them and walk in them, and I will be their God and they will be my people"* (2 Corinthians 6:16). I invite you to make my life Your dwelling place. Please occupy my life and be my God.

Please help me to be whole-hearted as I seek You this day, that this promise might become efficacious in my life: *"You will seek Me and find Me when you seek for Me with all your heart. I will be found by you"* (Jeremiah 29:13).

Jesus, You've also promised, *"I'm with you always, even to the end of the world"* (Matthew 28:20). I claim this wonderful promise in Your name right now and look forward to Your companionship throughout this day and until I see You coming in the clouds of heaven to take me home.

---

6    If I'm a new creation in Christ, why do I so often want to do the wrong thing? When you're "in Christ," you have new software—the mind of Christ. However, your hardware (your body and brain) will retain many of its old negative tendencies until Jesus returns and gives you a new body and brain.

If you're new at prayer, see *"Praying Yourself to Death"* on p. 159.

We've all been saved to serve. So go into your day now and find out who God wants to love through you.

# CHAPTER FIVE

# Dying for a Better Relationship

## (Being more self-effacing can be really helpful)

*I can't believe you just said that!*

*No way! You've got to be kidding!*

*That is so retarded!*

Ever said words like these to someone who said something you totally disagreed with?

Relationship guru John Gottman[1] says 69 percent of the issues all couples face in their relationships never get resolved.

This means if you're in a relationship, two-thirds of the issues you'll face ("*You never take the garbage out. You always leave dirty dishes in the sink. You overdrew the checking account again. You always make us late...*") will be irreconcilable. They won't get fixed.

Intriguingly, however, Gottman says the Masters of relationships do just fine despite neither partner ever coming around to the other's viewpoint. But the Disasters of relationships crash and burn (fight or break up).

Oh, by the way, where do you see yourself in this arena? Are you a

---

1.   Gottman wrote *The Seven Principles for Making Marriage Work* (New York, NY: Crown Publishers, 1999). He bases his statements on years of research in what he calls a Love Lab.

Master or a Disaster when it comes to your relationships? How well do you do in your relationship with your kids? Or if you don't have kids, how well do you do in your relationship with the people you work with? Or with your significant other?

I tell couples that I counsel, *"Love is not enough. Work at meeting your partner's primary relationship needs. Then tackle your differences."* Most couples I work with, by the way, admit they don't know their partner's top relationship needs. If you're in a couple relationship, do you know yours?

When I first met Diane seventeen years ago, I asked her what her primary relationship needs were. She replied, *"I need to be worshiped and adored."* I told her, *"I worship God, but I'm willing to adore you."* She replied, *"That'll work."* And so far it has.

What kind of relationship needs do you have? Most women say they want "to love and be loved," and men say they want to be respected. Intimacy both emotional and physical are high on most people's lists. Also, to feel **safe** with another is a biggie, as is the need to feel **valued**— to feel my partner has my back.

Of course, the needs list varies with the individual. One woman told me recently, *"I need words—words of appreciation, of affirmation, and an occasional 'I love you.' I need to feel accepted, not scrutinized. And I need lots of touching, too."* I told her, *"I'd like to be married to a woman like you."* Then I realized I was. It was Diane.

Relationship author Harville Hendrix[2] contends that most of us have relationship expectations at a subconscious level. What that means is that when we meet someone special, we drape our expectations over the other person, unaware that we're doing this. And, of course, the other person has no idea either about our expectations. We just expect the person to intuit our relationship needs and are majorly disappointed when they don't.

In the movie, *"Don Juan DeMarco,"* aging psychiatrist Marlon Brando has an epiphany when he's in his 70s and asks his wife of many years, Faye Dunaway, what her hopes and dreams were while he was pursuing his career. In the movie it appears they've been married for many years,

2.    Hendrix is the author of *Keeping the Love You Find* (New York, NY: Pocket Books, 1992).

so it's a great moment when she gets teary and replies, *"I thought you'd never ask."*

In case you've never asked—or not done so recently—may I suggest that you and your partner (if you have one) might inquire about each other's relationship needs now.

Equally important is the quality of a couple's friendship. The quality of a couple's friendship determines how successfully they'll get through their differences. Were you both good friends before you became lovers? If not, perhaps you should abandon your lovers mantra for a time and just see what it's like being friends. I contend that the combination of good friends first and lovers second makes for more successful relationships.

But let's switch gears now and examine some issues the two of you never get resolved? (*You drive too fast. You're always on the phone. You never pick up after yourself. You're too easy on the kids. You spend way too much money on...*). How well you do in the face of your issues will depend to what extent you're a relationship Master versus being a relationship Disaster. Wherever you are on the relationship scale, here are some points I hope you'll consider for your relationship differences.

1. **Just go along if it's not life-threatening**. Case in point. Diane and I are empty nesters, but she likes to shop at Costco. Ridiculous, I used to tell her, especially when it comes to purchasing produce. Because Costco only sells larger quantities, lots of our produce goes bad before the two of us can eat it.

   I used to complain somewhat loudly about this. Then I learned something. Shopping at Costco (one of her few indulgences) brings her a great deal of pleasure. So now I back off when she goes to Costco. Sometimes I even help her unload the car and lug in the 500-lb. buckets of kitty litter or potting soil that she brings home

2. **Try using humor to help with your issues.** Diane and I have a small relationship issue when it comes to eating. You see, I have a small mouth, and sometimes when eating I'll get a piece of food on my lips or at the corner of my mouth. And often—all of the time actually—Diane is pointing at the offending food particle so I can remove it.

   I tell her she doesn't need to do this—that I can usually feel the piece of food, and if she can delay saying anything for three to five seconds, I'll wipe my mouth. But Diane finds it difficult to do that, so we end up playing the "you've got food on your mouth" game again and again, occasionally in public and with friends.

A few months ago I decided to fight back—with humor. Diane and I were sitting in the cafeteria of the hospital where she works. A good friend had joined us, and I happened to have some cooked spinach on my plate. I waited until Diane was fully engaged in conversation with our friend before I made my move.

Then I placed a small amount of spinach on the tip of my nose. When she turned my way a few moments later, she fell for it. In the moment Diane pointed out the spinach, she knew she'd been had, and all three of us exploded in laughter. Now did this resolve the problem I've been citing? Of course not. But it did slow her down a little...I think.

Humor doesn't work with everyone when it comes to dealing with challenging issues, but humor can often help ease tensions when its devoid of teasing or putdowns.

3. **Learn to do repair attempts.** Repair attempts are a secret weapon for overcoming the acrimony that often emanates when we're exchanging very differing viewpoints. A repair attempt can be anything from a *"Hey, I think I got a little loud during our last exchange"* to a simple *"I'm sorry."* Bringing in a flower from the yard (even a dandelion can work) or saying, *"Want to go to TCBY—I'll buy?"* are examples of repair attempts.

   *But repair attempts are only useful if they work.* And let me tell you, when a couple can't find successful repair attempts, their relationship is in trouble. For more helpful information on repair attempts, I recommend John Gottman's *The Seven Principles for Making Marriage Work.* Even if you're not married, the principles he presents should be helpful.

4. **Choose to have low horizontal expectations.** By now you know you and your partner won't agree on every topic, so ease up even when you know you're right. *Even when I'm right?* Yes, especially when you're right. About being right, my pastor friend, Clarence

Schilt, says, *"We tend to sin more when we're right and right is not happening."* So once you've made your point, why do you have to control the outcome? Do you always have to be right? Why not give your partner permission to be wrong once in a while! Now isn't that a novel idea!

5. **Be respectful when you disagree.** When you and your partner are getting nowhere on some issue, it's okay to tell him or her, *"I think you're really wrong about this."* But add quickly, *"However, I respect your right to see it differently than I do."* Once you've blended respect into the mix, you should be able to move on—comfortably—your difference of opinion notwithstanding.

6. **Pray (silently) when the matter is not resolvable.** Oh, you're not the praying type? Well, then, don't pray. But let me share this anecdote with you. Once when Diane was going off on something I did (I threw out one of her half-dead plants without asking her first), I told her I couldn't believe we were even discussing such a mundane matter. She assured me we were having such a discussion. Finally, in a brilliant stroke, I shut up, prayed silently for God's intervention and watched Him intervene. And He really did, perhaps because I finally shut my mouth. By the next morning, we were good again.

One more thought on the matter of prayer. When your partner is really upset about a matter, it's usually a dumb idea to say, *"Let's pray about this."* It's a bad idea because it's bad timing, and your partner will probably think you're a hypocrite trying to use God to win the battle. Praying silently is fine. Just do it in your closet. Prayer can be powerful if you're both spiritual people, but not if you're using it to win your case.

Now I'd like to share with you a point that I think is huge for any couple who want to enhance their relationship. I hope you'll reflect on it carefully. The points that follow should be helpful, but this first one I've never heard or read about in a relationship seminar or book. And I will posit here that unless you're hooked up with a sociopath, this point may be my greatest gift to you in this book.[3]

---

3. The Exchanged Life is described in detail in chapter 4.

## Enhance All of Your Relationships By Obtaining a Brand-new Self

Having an alive self is one of the greatest threats against your having a successful and fulfilling relationship. Mostly, self is ugly. There's a hurt self, an offended self, an impatient self, an unforgiving self, self-pity, an outraged or angry self, a bitter self, even a righteous self, as in righteous (often *unrighteous*) indignation. We usually don't like folks who are full of themselves. Process Point #1 here every day, and you'll be able to implement those that follow much more readily.

1. **Start your day right. Exchange your old self for a new self!** Emptied of self, you'll enhance all of your relationships and be able to cool your jets when differences arise. The Bible says to *"put off your old self which is being corrupted by its deceitful desires...and put on the new self created to be like God"* (Ephesians 4:22, 24).

   You can become emptied of self (a change of nature) by choosing to do so first thing every morning and asking the Holy Spirit to make your decision a reality. Doing this should help you be less defensive and more able to hear your partner and be responsive to his/her needs. (Review chapter 4 for help doing this).

2. **Love is never enough.** So learn to meet needs. Do you know your partner's primary relationship needs? Even if thirty years have gone by, it's never too late to ask.

3. **Get your sleep.** Seven to eight hours for most of us, and you'll be nicer to be with.

4. **Friends first.** The quality of a couples' friendship always determines how the relationship will go. This could be a problem if you started off as hot lovers. You might need to develop a friendship now if you're up to it and get out of the hot-lovers mode.

5. **Ask for grace every day.** Grace is God's power made perfect in weakness—and your key to a more balanced life. *"My grace is sufficient for you,"* He promises. And it really is because we're all weak in certain areas (such as remembering anniversaries, being on time, in controlling our mouths, thinking about your partner first, etc.).

6.  **Never retaliate**. Instead, look to see what's driving your pain if he/she unloads on you.

7.  **Have low horizontal expectations** (even the nicest folks will let you down sometimes).

8.  **Have high vertical expectations** (God will never let you down if you choose to trust Him).

9.  **Have a realistic budget. And work hard at staying out of debt.** Issues with finance, sex, religion, and in-laws are the Top Four of all relationship busters. But financial issues beat all the others when it comes to the degrading of relationships. So live within your means and remember that God has promised to meet ALL your needs. (Philippians 4:19). DaveRamsey.com might be helpful also if you need to get your finances in order.

10. **Don't be too needy**. High-maintenance people wear out their partner. They simply can't have successful relationships. (If that's you, spend time in chapter 4.)

11. **Stay well.** It's tough to have a successful relationship with someone who is perennially unwell (unless you were born to be a caretaker).

12. **No relationship is ever 50-50. So give 100 percent.** And don't worry about who does more.

13. **Do something fun that you both enjoy, with some regularity** (annually won't cut it).

14. **Don't stonewall.** Stay open. Pay attention. Listen. Maybe your partner's got a point. Stonewalling is one of the Four Horsemen of the Apocalypse for relationships—and men do it most.

15. **Don't be critical even when the other one is (and women do it most).** Never say, *"You always...You never..."* If you have to say something negative, do it like this: *"Can I tell you how it makes me feel when such and such happens between us?"*

16. **Practice thoughtfulness.** Do the little things, especially little things you know he/she appreciates.

17. **Keep courting, dating.** Like maybe a date this weekend? (Okay, maybe it's Friday. How about next week!)

18. **Practice patience**. Patience is a huge gift for all successful relationships. The Exchanged Life (see chapter 4) will be essential if you're a naturally impatient person. It's one of the natural fruits of the Exchanged Life. Go for it, even if it takes you the rest of your life.

19. **Don't flirt.** Flirting with others if you're in a relationship is stupid, hurtful, and immature. Don't do it!

20. **Use humor very carefully.** Avoid wisecracks, teasing, putdowns. Let your humor be self-deprecating and never at your partner's expense, or don't try to be funny.

21. **Suture your mouth.** There is a wonderful power in silence when everything is breaking loose. Claim promises like: *"The Lord will fight for you, and you have only to be still"* (Exodus 14:14).

22. **Six of the smartest words ever spoken: *"I'm sorry. Will you forgive me?"*** Use them (not just the first two, but all six, especially if your offense caused pain), and your relationship will prosper. And even when you're sure you're right, just say, *"I'm sorry that what I said made you feel bad."*

23. **Be respectful, even when you disagree.** Sixty-nine percent of all relationship issues are not resolvable, as I mentioned earlier, but the Masters of relationships do just fine despite their differences. **Example:** Rather than say, *"You're full of it,"* try something like this: *"Honey, I think your view on this is incorrect, but I respect your right to see it differently than I do."* Then drop it. Maybe tomorrow one or both of you will see things differently—and maybe you won't (and it won't matter anyway).

24. **Make eye contact and hug.** Make eye contact like you did on your first date when you couldn't take your eyes off each other. I'm always saddened when I see older couples in a restaurant chowing down, barely talking, and not making eye contact with each other. Hey, and don't forget to hug either. Hugs and warm eye contact are wonderful relationship enhancers. Use them often whatever your age.

---

*From a seminar by Mike Jones at a recent men's conference. Reach Mike at mjonespdx1@gmail.com.*

# CHAPTER SIX

# The Devil Made Me Do It!

Your chances of having something bad happen—of being taken advantage of, mugged, wrongfully fired, hit with a nuisance lawsuit, being in a car accident, needing emergency surgery, dealing with some sort of abuse or domestic violence, enduring anxiety disorder or depression, or being attacked by some new virus—is extremely high living on this planet.

That's because we're living in a war zone!

Speaking of getting mugged, when I was in graduate school in Washington, D.C., I stopped one night at a red light on my way to class. Suddenly, five or six guys came out of the shadows and surrounded my car. Quickly I gunned my car engine loudly, made sure no cars were coming; then, as the guys in front fell back, I ran the red light and escaped.

It's a war zone out there.

What the devil is going on? you may ask. That brings me to the point of this chapter. Because, you see, although a number of churches today view Satan as a metaphor for evil, the Bible identifies him as real. Scripture describes the devil as the culprit who has turned our planet into a war zone. The devil is alive and well on Planet Earth. He's real, invisible, and works behind the scenes to cause a lot of our problems, including problems between nations. The Bible also tells us that the problem of evil first began in heaven, of all places.

*There was war in heaven. Michael and his angels fought against the dragon, and the dragon and his angels fought back. But he was not strong enough, and they lost their place in heaven. The great dragon was hurled down—that ancient serpent called the devil, or Satan, who leads the whole world astray. He was hurled to the earth, and his angels with him* (Revelation 12:7-9).

You need to understand this, because the news media almost never offers a biblical understanding to life's challenges. Every time a mass shooting or something else awful happens, the media will go for days trying to determine the motives of whoever committed some atrocity. Usually that search is futile, especially if the perpetrator is dead. The fact that earth is host to a literal devil and millions of fallen angels, all seeking our destruction, is never mentioned, although the Bible does. But who takes the Bible seriously anymore?

It is interesting that the Bible never provides an explanation for evil except to call it a mystery—*"the mystery of iniquity"* (2 Thessalonians 2:7).

In fact, according to the Bible, the devil once served God much like the president's press secretary. His original name was Lucifer, which means "light bearer." Until he went into rebellion, Lucifer communicated messages from God to the angels and to the entire universe. After he fell, Lucifer was renamed Satan, which means "adversary of God."

The prophet Isaiah refers to the devil's fall in these words:

*How you are fallen from heaven, O Lucifer, son of the morning! How you are cut down to the ground. . . . For you have said in your heart: 'I will ascend into heaven, I will exalt my throne above the stars of God. . . . I will be like the Most High'"* (Isaiah 14:12-14).

After perhaps thousands of years of service to God—the Bible doesn't say how many—Lucifer became jealous of Jesus and began to entertain doubts about God's goodness. He was subtle and deceitful when he first began trying to undermine God. He cleverly insinuated doubts among the angels about God's goodness. As a result, like a growing cancer, discontent slowly began to infect the angels. Finally open rebellion broke out, and as I noted earlier, Satan launched the first war in the universe.

Of course he lost. The Bible says that a third of the angels of heaven were lost with him. They were banished to the earth where Lucifer, now called the devil, deceived our first parents into rebelling against their Creator. We've been paying the price ever since. Because even though we were created to live forever, no one gets out of here alive.

With all the hell that has broken loose on this planet, it's amazing to me that 60 percent to 70 percent of Americans, including a majority of professing Christians, do not believe in a literal devil. Most people just laugh when someone says, *"The devil made me do it."*

The Bible, however, takes the existence of the devil quite seriously. Jesus tangled with him throughout His ministry. And Jesus' disciple Peter warned, *"Your enemy the devil prowls around like a roaring lion looking for someone to devour"* (1 Peter 5:8).

How does the devil devour people?

Author Ron Halvorsen, in his book, *Prayer Warriors,* says the devil eats people up with *"fear, guilt, shame, self-condemnation, depression, feelings of hopelessness, helplessness, worthlessness."*[1] These are some of the devil's most frequently used weapons. Halvorsen adds to the list both poverty and prosperity, sexual desire misused, the need for acceptance, and preoccupation with pleasure, recreation, and career success.

I believe the devil also works through mental illness, both causing it and capitalizing on it when it's already present.

By the way, in a devastating statement, the Bible tells us that apart from Christ we can be *"taken captive by the devil at his will"* (2 Timothy 2:26).

Hard to believe? Well let me ask you: Have you ever done or said something that was so out of character for you that you could hardly believe it yourself? *"I can't believe I said that—or did that,"* we may say to ourselves afterward. *"I wasn't myself."* And, indeed, that may have been the case.

Canadian Roger Morneau was heavily recruited by a group of demon worshipers before becoming a Christian. Later he wrote a book exposing some of the devil's tactics.[2] And one of these tactics, he says, is to

---

1. Ron Halverson, *Prayer Warriors* (Fallbrook, CA: Hart Research Center, 1995).

2. Roger Morneau, A *Trip Into the Supernatural* (Hagerstown, MD: Review and Herald Publishing Association, 1993).

insinuate a terrible thought into someone's mind, causing that person to believe he or she must be really awful to have had such a thought—when it really wasn't theirs in the first place. Can you imagine the horror of that happening?

Well, there's a good possibility this may already have happened to you, perhaps even going back to your childhood. Wouldn't childhood be a logical place for an enemy like Satan to plant corrupt thoughts and ideas? Can you see what an inconceivable advantage the devil has over those who disbelieve his existence? Perhaps this is where some of our own compulsions or obsessions had their origin.

I'd like to add here that I am also suspicious that some of our *dreams* may be devil-produced. Consider this letter to a newspaper advice columnist as a possible example:

> *I am a male in my early twenties. I have never had any sexual interest in men. Even though my relationships with women have been few and far between, I have always been attracted to them.*
>
> *Recently I had a dream that I was with another man. Since then I have been very confused. My sex drive has diminished, and I find I am questioning my sexual orientation.*
>
> *I have no desire to be with a man, but the fact that I had a dream like that has left me flustered and wondering how something like that could have come into my head.*

The columnist, presumably without a biblical worldview, had no good answer and suggested that he come up with his own interpretation of the dream, perhaps with the help of a therapist.[3]

Now I don't believe for a minute that all of our dreams are devil-produced. But I am personally convinced that some are. And how devastating this has to be for the person who doesn't have a clue about what might really be going on!

So what is a person to do who doesn't want the devil's control but would like to have God's protection? The good news is that God has promised protection for those who have a relationship with Him. Listen to some of His promises:

---

3.     From the "Ask Amy" advice column published by the *Chicago Tribune*, February, 2007.

*I am your shield, your very great reward* (Genesis 15:1).

*The name of the Lord is a strong tower; the righteous run to it and are safe* (Proverbs 18:10).

*The angel of the Lord encamps around those who fear him, and he delivers them* (Psalm 34:7).

*I give you power . . . over all the power of the enemy* (Luke 10:19).

*When the enemy shall come in like a flood, the Spirit of the Lord will raise up a standard against him* (Isaiah 59:19).

*Submit yourselves, then, to God. Resist the devil, and he will flee from you* (James 4:7).

These promises are for the Christian to claim. Are you a Christian, by the way? Go back to the protocols in chapter 4 if you'd like to remind yourself what is involved.

I share the following anecdote to help illustrate how Jesus helps us in our battles with an adversary far more powerful than we are.

Some years ago, a single friend of mine was out country-western dancing when someone took exception to him on the dance floor. He never did learn why. Now my friend was no spring chicken. He was in his 50s and not very big. And the fellow who was unhappy with him was much younger and considerably bigger than he was. So the outcome of a physical encounter was never seriously in doubt.

But in his moment of extremity, my friend turned quickly to someone nearby whom he knew. That friend's name was Andre. He was a handsome young African-American man who was about six feet tall and a muscular 220 pounds. *"Andre, this guy here seems to have a problem with me,"* my friend called out. Andre was in front of him in an instant. *"You've got a problem with my friend?"* he asked the young guy.

*"No, sir. No problem at all,"* the fellow replied, taking one look at Andre looming over him and beating a hasty retreat.

The next time you have a problem with your adversary, the devil, just ask your Best Friend Jesus for some assistance. The Bible records that Jesus has had plenty of scraps with Satan, and He's defeated him every time. He promises you and me, *"The Lord will fight for you; you have only to be still"* (Exodus 14:14). Such a deal if we can remember to take advantage of the offer!

Before I experienced God in my life, I suffered from two major addictions—an addiction to cigarettes and a love addiction that led me to have affairs. (In chapters 2 and 3 I tell how Jesus transformed my life in these areas.) Regular infusions of God's grace (a wondrous element of the Godhead) in my life enabled me to overcome my addictions after I asked God to replace me.

Daily infusions of grace in your life will help you to overcome your addictions as well. You see, when we accept God into our lives, His grace not only empowers us, it also satisfies us so profoundly at our core that our addictions weaken and begin to lose their power over us.

And the more we hang with Jesus, the less power they have in our lives. Is the devil really involved in our addictions? you may ask. I believe that often he is. The danger of indulging an addictive fantasy is that over time the highs aren't as good as they used to be. Addictions and fantasies are progressive, in a negative way. So to get the high that we crave, there's a real danger that our thought life will worsen and that some of us might actually carry out our snakebit fantasies.

The underlying problem with addictions is that they become objects of worship—false gods, if you will. And when we worship counterfeit gods, we break the first of God's Ten Commandments—the one that talks about not worshiping any other god except our Creator. *And have no doubt about this, it's our nature to worship something, even if it's ourselves.*

How can experiencing God's grace be a counterpoint to an addiction? Well, for one thing, God has promised to satisfy our desires with good things (see Psalm 103:5). (Keep in mind that even God can't satisfy the needs of anyone when the natural self is alive and well.) That's why dying to self every day is the place to begin. And why Jesus urges us to *"seek first his [God's] kingdom and his righteousness, and all these things will be given to you as well"* (Matthew 6:33).

The apostle Paul adds this promise: *"My God will meet all your needs according to his glorious riches in Christ Jesus"* (Philippians 4:19). Claim these promises when you're feeling weak, when you're feeling empty and listless, or when you're being tempted, and watch what happens.

I also love God's promise in Psalm 145:16, which says that He's willing to *"satisfy the desires of every living thing."* I claim it often lest I try to satisfy my desires in an unhealthy way.

By the way, I contend that God never matches the devil's highs that come to us through wrong-doing and addictive behaviors. Instead, He offers us peace and satisfaction along with His grace and love. He also promises to satisfy our desires with good things for as long as we live and to give us the desires of our hearts.[4]

So which would you rather have—an addiction which gives the devil control of your life and that will eventually kill you, or God's peace, love, joy, and satisfaction at your core?

That's a no-brainer, isn't it? (Actually that depends on which side of your brain you're working from—the rational left or the irrational right side that is driven by feelings.)

By the way, if you've been perplexed over the meanings of the Mark of the Beast versus the Seal of God described in the book of Revelation, may I suggest there may well be a simpler answer than those provide who believe in a literal answer.

*Rather than a literal seal or mark, I suggest that the Seal of God primarily means an unselfish, loving character* (Galatians 5:22, 23) *punctuated by obedience to God's principles.* And the Mark of the Beast mostly centers on a rebellious life, or—*"I do things my way. I'd like to have God's input, but I'll make the call, thank you."*

The person with the godly seal is rebellion-free and safe to save. The person with the satanic mark isn't. It's just about that simple.

You and I are living in a war zone. But with Jesus **in** our lives—with Jesus **as** our life—we can make it safely through the devil's minefields and emerge victoriously from every battle. Jesus says, *"Behold, I give you power. . . over all the power of the enemy"* (Luke 10:19).

And that's a promise worth obtaining every day!

**Some strategies for successfully coping with Satan's tactics and defeating them:**

---

4.   *"Who satisfies you with good for as long as you live." "Take delight in the Lord, and He will give you the desires of your heart."* (Psalm 103:5 and 37:4).

**Satan's tactics.** Satan can't read our minds, but he can put his thoughts there.[5] Invisible, he has caused 60 percent to 70 percent of Christians to disbelieve his existence. He is a master at working our feelings, causing us to feel anxious, inadequate, and depressed.

As I mentioned earlier, one of his most successful tactics is to provoke discord and dissension between people and between nations.

Satan is well organized and controls the minds of millions of fallen angels, now called demons. The Bible describes Satan as walking around seeking victims to devour (1 Peter 5:8) and also as sometimes masquerading as an angel of light (2 Corinthians 11:14). One way he devours people is to eat them up with negative feelings, compulsions, and obsessions.

The devil is real, he is angry, and he is constantly on the attack, often through the "D words": *deception, depression, doubt, discord, dismay, disbelief, dilemmas, distractions, degraded thinking, delusion, dissension, and diversion.*

Here are some weapons God has placed in our hands to defeat the devil.

**Realize what may be going on**. When there is discord between you and someone else, for instance, recognize that the devil may be at work. Understand that more may be going on than just the person who is causing you grief. Satan may be involved, as well. Then rely on God's Word as Jesus did to defeat him.

**Claim God's promises.** We've looked at a number of the promises God gives us in His Word. Here are two more: *"For he himself is our peace, who has made the two one and has broken down the dividing wall of hostility. . . so making peace and might reconcile us both to God in one body through the cross, thereby bringing the hostility to an end"* (Ephesians 2:14-16.) *"Submit yourselves, therefore, to God. Resist the devil, and he will flee from you"* (James 4:7).

---

5.     *"Your Thoughts—Are They Your Own?"* from Roger Morneau, *More Incredible Answers to Prayer* (Hagerstown, MD: Review and Herald Publishing Association, 1993). Before becoming a Christian, the author was heavily recruited by satanic agencies when he was a younger man.

**Ask God to fight for you**. He has promised to fight our battles if we will allow him to. *"The Lord will fight for you, and you have only to be still"* (Exodus 14:14).

**Obtain a new self daily.** *"Put off your old self, which is being corrupted by its deceitful desires; and . . . put on the new self, created to be like God in true righteousness and holiness"* (Ephesians 4:22-24). Make this choice every morning, and the Holy Spirit will make your decision a reality. The new self will not be responsive to Satan's temptations; your old self always will.

Besides our own corrupted nature, Satan and his demons are our most powerful adversaries. But Jesus defeated Satan and his hosts at the Cross. Satan is deceptive and powerful, but God's Word renders him impotent. Practice meeting his attacks with Scripture just as Jesus did.

Here is an example. When Diane and I were hopelessly lost in Paris recently, we could easily have given each other a bad time for the other's contribution to being lost. However, we often claim this Scripture in times of difficulty, and we did so this time: *"All things work together for good to them who trust the Lord, and are called according to His purpose"* (Romans 8:28).

In this instance, as darkness fell, we continued to struggle. Then we met an amazing Parisian couple who personally escorted us through a complicated series of subway rides, walking us the final blocks until we were just a short distance from our hotel. We told them as we hugged them goodbye that they were angels. Perhaps they were.

The apostle Paul counsels us,

*"Finally, be strong in the Lord and in his mighty power. Put on the full armor of God so that you can take your stand against the devil's schemes. For our struggle is not against flesh and blood, but against . . . the powers of this dark world and against the spiritual forces of evil in the heavenly realms. Therefore put on the full armor of God, so that when the day of evil comes, you may be able to stand your ground, and after you have done everything, to stand"* (Ephesians 6:10-13).

(Note: Read verses 14-17 for a description of all the pieces of God's armor. Put your armor on every morning).

Finally, keep in mind that God's promises are more powerful than speeding bullets. They are devastating to Satan. Use them!

# CHAPTER SEVEN

# Why Modern Christianity Doesn't Cut It!

**W**hen Adam and Eve sold out to Satan, God's adversary and former top angel in heaven, human nature crashed as we all inherited his nature. Jesus referred to Satan as a liar and murderer. He told the religious leaders of His time that their father was the devil.[1] Get the point? He's your father, too.

At the dawn of time, Earth's first family took on Satan's DNA, evidenced most painfully when Cain murdered his brother, Abel. And all over the planet we've been killing each other ever since, nearly 18,000 in the U.S. alone every year. And of course, because we're snakebit, most of our relationships are challenging, too, as the high rates of disillusionment and divorce attest.

Even youngsters aren't immune. A few days ago I read about a 12-year-old who shot and killed his dad while he slept, then several days later about a third-grader writing death threats to his classmates.

Up until the last fifteen years, I didn't understand that if I wanted a transformed self, my current self had to die. This isn't a physical death—it's an exchange of the natural self for a supernatural self. It's not a better me—it's a different me. Or as Jesus put it, we actually cross over from death to life—life as it is in the Godhead. (See John 5:24.)

Traditional Christianity says to accept Jesus, clean up your act, and

---

1.    *"You are children of your father the devil"* (John 8:44).

start going to church. Regrettably, that doesn't work when it comes to transformation, as you'll see shortly.

Here's what does work, according to Jesus: *"If anyone would follow Me, let him deny himself and take up his cross daily and follow Me"* (Luke 9:23). Did you notice that Jesus said this must be a daily experience? Get self out of your life daily, and you won't be full of yourself. Instead, you'll have room for Jesus. *"It's no longer I who live, but Christ who lives in me"* (Galatians 2:20).

What I didn't hear in churches I attended was that transformation must be a daily experience or I'll lose it. *It's wonderful to have made a Christian commitment last year or back in 1998, but what about this morning?* This daily renewal is essential because your old snakebit nature is always trying to make a comeback.

In the absence of this, even the nicest among us are capable of irrational thinking. Ever had the urge to kill? Once during a bleak time in my life I briefly fantasized about taking out a lawyer and his client who had threatened to bring a nuisance lawsuit against me, possibly bringing down my fledgling business unless I did what they wanted.

Thinking of killing them was crazy, you say, and I didn't linger long on the thought. But at the time I was living a hardscrabble existence running my business out of an apartment where I was living alone, taking almost no salary, and driving an old beater of a car. I was outraged at the threat. But here's my point: All of us on this planet are afflicted with a certain amount of insanity whether we act on our irrational thoughts or not, and, tragically, some of us do, as you may have noticed in the news recently.

If you permit your old self to have life, you have Mad Cow Disease of the soul. And while the results may play out differently in different lives, still there's no antivenin for this illness other than to become a different person (you choose to make the exchange, and the Holy Spirit makes it happen). I can't stress how important this is.

You see, if you don't process this experience daily, you can try for all you're worth to be a decent person, but sooner or later you'll crash and burn. This is why a majority of Christians, according to demographer George Barna, act no differently than those who make no profession of

Christianity. They may believe in God and go to church, but they don't have a daily change at their core.

As I noted earlier, the Bible underscores the problem in words like these: *"The heart is deceitful above all things and desperately corrupt, incurable, who can understand it?"* (Jeremiah 17:9). And *"the whole head is sick"* (Isaiah 1:5).

Demographer Barna has reported for years that getting baptized and attending church most Sundays doesn't cut it when it comes to living a transformed life. A friend of mine who's in church most Sundays told me recently about his previously immoral lifestyle and said he has no regrets about his many conquests.

So let me ask you, Do you think all these folks are going to heaven who confess Jesus but often live like the devil—or at least think like him? (Some 95 percent of men and women in the U.S. admit to indulging illicit sexual fantasies.) Some churches answer Yes. Once you've made a Christian decision, you're in, no matter what your lifestyle or thought-style, they say.

Jesus apparently didn't see it that way. He said, *"Narrow is the road that leads to life, and only a few find it"* (Matthew 7:14). And the apostle Paul warned about the possibility of falling away even after a Christian commitment, pointing out, concerning himself, *"I keep under my body ...lest...when I have preached to others, I myself should be a castaway"* (1 Corinthians 9:27).

*"Just say a few correct words and you're saved"* also bothered Matt Casper, an atheist featured with Jim Henderson, a pastor, in the book, *Jim and Casper Go to Church.* Henderson paid Casper to attend some of America's best-known Christian churches with him, including Rick Warren's, and to report his observations. What bothered Casper most was the idea of saying a prayer, accepting Jesus, and you're in. *"Shouldn't there be more to it than that?"* he asks. *"Is this what Jesus told you guys to do?"*

Well, actually no. Jesus never said, *"Just believe in Me, and I'll see you in heaven."* However, He did tell the Jewish religious leader, Nicodemus, *"You must be born again"* (John 3:7). And He also talked a lot about love—even loving one's enemies. He also stressed the importance of keeping His commandments. *"If you love Me, keep My commandments"* (Luke 9:23; John 14:15). *"Whoever says I know Him, but doesn't keep His Commandments is a liar"* (1 John 2:4).

*So what's genuine Christianity all about? It's a call to die to everything nasty, prideful, and rebellious about yourself (the natural self) and then be rebirthed as a different (think supernatural) being daily.* And if you're thinking, *That will be the death of me,* you're on to something.

I missed that during my early years. I believed in Jesus, but I didn't know Him. I didn't have the *experience* of Christianity—really *knowing* God—until much later when I finally understood what Jesus meant when He said: *"And this is life eternal that they might **know** you, the only true God, and Jesus Christ whom He has sent"* (John 17:3).

*By the way, this is an amazing relationship that transcends the intimacy of sex.*

Every relationship in your life should be subservient to this one. Which means it requires some one-on-one time with God every day. And certainly that means more than a quick morning prayer and out the door. I find modern Christianity rarely models how to experience the Exchanged Life. This is why most Christians are, regrettably, like everybody else.[2]

---

2.    For more detail on areas where modern Christian churches are no longer biblical, go to *Appendix: Preparing to Meet Jesus,* on p. 153.

# CHAPTER EIGHT

# How to Survive a Crisis

On Sept. 10, 1974, in Kinshasha, Zaire (now called the Congo), one of the greatest heavyweight boxing fights of all time took place. I allude to it here because it provides a lesson on how to get through a crisis. Now I'm no fan of boxing, but this fight has something important to teach us.

The contestants were George Foreman and Muhammad Ali. Foreman was a 25-year-old who had knocked out every opponent who had come up against him, while Muhammad Ali, now in his 30s, was thought to be past his prime. In fact, Ali went into the contest as an 8-to-1 underdog.

A boxing match between heavyweights is a classic example of a crisis. Because the goal is either to destroy or be destroyed.

Most of the world's great sportswriters were on hand for the event, but few of them gave Ali much chance of winning. In fact, some were concerned about his survival. One wrote that shortly before the fight, Ali's dressing room was like a morgue. *"The sense was,"* he wrote, *"that we were watching a man going out to the gallows."*

Even Ali's own entourage was terrified. So fearsome was George Foreman's reputation that most thought that Ali would be terribly hurt or possibly even killed in the fight. Ali too seemed to sense the mood. He tried to lift the spirits of his entourage by telling them, *"I'm going to dance, and that man will be bewildered."* Then he asked them, *"What am I going to do?"*

And they replied, *"You're going to dance."* But they were crying even as they said the words.

In the first round, instead of dancing or running, Ali came out fighting. In fact, he threw twelve right-hand leads to Foreman's head, something that professional boxers never do. And before the end of the first round, Foreman went crazy and launched a two-fisted attack on Ali.

Ali survived. But at the end of the first round, one long-time boxing writer said this was the only time he had ever seen Ali with fear in his eyes. He was up against a younger, stronger man who was unstoppable. Another writer wrote, *"The nightmare that had been awaiting him in the ring was finally here."*

Ali sat on his stool for the one-minute rest between rounds with a mixture of fear and horror on his face. Then he kind of nodded to himself as if to say, *"Got to get it together. You've really got to get it together."* Another writer recalled, *"It was as if he were looking into the eyes of his Maker."*

But during those sixty seconds before the second round, Ali realized he wasn't going to get through this crisis with his fists alone. Ali has never said what came to his mind, but we know what he did. He defied all logic and largely went into a defensive mode.

During the next four rounds, he allowed Foreman to pound on him mercilessly. But he absorbed the pounding—not by dancing, but by lying against the ropes, ducking, blocking punches, and fighting back only occasionally.

As the fight progressed, Ali began talking to Foreman when the two were tied up. He said, *"George, you disappoint me. I thought you could punch harder than that. George, you don't punch harder than popcorn!"*

Enraged, out-of-control, Foreman continued to throw punches, mostly without Ali fighting back very often. His corner was horrified, and boxing pundits thought that the end had come for Ali. However, by the end of the fifth round, onlookers began to see that Ali might actually have a strategy. Foreman had worn himself out, and Ali was still standing.

In the seventh and eighth rounds, Ali began fighting back more. Then with thirty seconds left in the eighth round, Ali suddenly struck with fury. He threw a series of punches to Foreman's jaw, and Big George, weakened from his out-of-control pummeling of Ali, fell to the canvas.

He wouldn't beat the count. Muhammad Ali's crisis was over. Once again, he was the heavyweight boxing champion of the world.

As I said earlier, I don't have any love for boxing. However, a boxing match does provide a good example of a crisis at a primitive level. And even though we may never get anywhere near a boxing ring ourselves, the results of how we handle our own personal crisis can often be just as devastating as a knockout punch if we don't make good decisions.

## What You Should Know About LCUs

In a now-famous study begun in 1967, Doctors Thomas Holmes and Richard Rahe examined the stress created by a variety of crises. They assigned a descending value, ranging from 100 "life-changing units"— or LCUs—for a major crisis (death of a spouse) down to a value of 11 LCUs for a minor one (getting a traffic ticket). Also high on the list of difficult crises to handle was divorce (73 LCUs), death of a close family member (63 LCUs), losing one's job (47 LCUs), and business or financial problems (38 and 39 LCUs).

Based on these numbers—essentially an indication of how many crises a person has had within a certain length of time—the researchers were able to determine the likelihood of that person having a stress-related illness or accident. An accumulated LCU value between 150 and 300 puts a person's chances of having an accident or illness within two years at 51 percent. If the LCU value exceeds 300, the likelihood of accident or illness rises to 80 percent.

You might think about that if you're going through a really rough patch just now.

Had any significant crises in your life lately? Let's take a look at a small sampling of common crises. How many can you identify with?

- ▸ Your car won't start.
- ▸ The cool kids at school snicker when you walk by.
- ▸ You find yourself in an abusive relationship.
- ▸ Someone you've been dating but don't love, proposes.

- ▶ You overdraw your checking account.

- ▶ You get laid off at work. Fired, in other words.

- ▶ Your grandchildren come to visit—for a month.

- ▶ Your car is rear-ended.

- ▶ Your 3-year-old says, *"I hate you."*

- ▶ Your kids won't stop fighting.

- ▶ You're forced to file for bankruptcy.

- ▶ You flunk your final exams.

- ▶ Someone you love says, *"I need some space—I'm moving out."*

- ▶ Someone vandalizes your mailbox, your car, your body.

- ▶ You begin having some uncertainty that God exists.

- ▶ You've had a persistent internal pain—for three weeks.

- ▶ The baby's sick again.

- ▶ You're heading into a war zone *(that could include coming home from work)*.

Any of these sound familiar?

Ever had a crisis in your life that never seemed to end? It went on and on and on—for weeks, for months, perhaps longer. What do you do with a crisis that just won't quit?

David Jacobsen, a former hostage in Lebanon, tells how he kept his sanity while caged like an animal and clad only in his underwear for seventeen months. He lists ten coping mechanisms he used. At the top of his list? Belief in God and prayer. Following these were believing in one's own strength, faith that the crisis will end favorably, thoughts of loved ones, and a sense of humor.

Here are ten coping mechanisms for your consideration if you're facing a crisis:

1. **Cultivate a sense of humor**. Those who can maintain their sense of humor during the worst of times are far more likely to survive a crisis than those who can't or won't. This is not to suggest that

we take life-or-death situations lightly. Instead, avoid taking life so seriously that you allow bad things to immobilize you or to knock you into depression.

When one of his kidnappers held a gun to the back of Jacobsen's neck and said, *"You dead,"* Jacobsen responded, *"This is Tuesday night, and I still have a lot of work to do before you shoot me. Tomorrow is a full schedule of appointments. But Thursday afternoon I have time to die."*

The kidnapper swore at him in Arabic and left the room. Maintaining a sense of humor can be a real safety valve during difficult times. The Bible tells us that *"a merry heart does us good like a medicine"* (Proverbs 17:22). (I'm not suggesting you not take it seriously if somebody has a gun pointed at you.)

2. **Practice crisis prevention by thinking before you speak.** Easier said than done, I know. But an argument with your spouse or another significant person in your life can lead to harsh words. Harsh words may not always be relationship threatening, but they can be relationship diminishing. Why let that happen? So practice thinking before you speak.

   After all, how helpful will it be if you tell her she's an airhead or him that he's an idiot? The Bible says, *"A gentle answer turns away wrath, but a harsh word stirs up anger"* (Proverbs 15:1). And *"He who guards his mouth and his tongue keeps himself from calamity"* (Proverbs 21:23).

   I always try to pray before discussing significant issues with my spouse, especially finances, which is one of the four horsemen of relationship apocalypses.

   I've even trained myself to breathe a quick prayer before answering the phone. I try to remember to seek wisdom and grace to handle the call appropriately and have come to believe that prayer helps me be nicer to telephone solicitors.

3. **Be sure that God is really in charge**. Either you're in charge of your life or God is. If you're in charge, you'll look to yourself—and likely get in trouble. I had a friend whose wife was unhappy with him because, as she put it, *"You're always right, aren't you?"* But

he said to me, *"Mike, what am I to do? I usually **am** right."* If God's in charge, you'll probably bring more humility to the table—even when you're right.

4. **Look to God whenever you're facing a crisis**. Isn't this just a formula? It sure is. It's a supernatural formula. As Peter found out, some who look to Jesus even end up walking on water. In the same way, other Bible characters learned that they could walk through fire and not be burned. You'll be amazed how often you get through a crisis when you look to God for His guidance and intervention instead of to yourself.

   God said it would be this way when you rely on Him: *"When you walk through the fire, you will not be burned"* (Isaiah 43:2, 3). So start training yourself *now to look to God.* Then when the next crisis strikes, you'll be okay even when you shouldn't be. Hey, you'll never know unless you try it.

5. **Trust God's promises when you are in crisis**. After all, He's promised to supply your every need (see Philippians 4:19). He's also promised to *"fight for you; you need only to be still"* (Exodus 14:14). Jesus also said He'd give you power over *"all the power of the enemy"* (Luke 10:19). (So with His protection, maybe you really don't need to pack a gun?) As I've noted earlier, God's also on record as promising to give you *"the desires of your heart"* if you trust Him (Psalm 37:4).

   I was with a friend, Ron, the night he received a rejection letter from the medical school to which he had applied. A political power play by someone connected with the school appeared to be sacrificing his admission so someone with lesser qualifications could get in. As the two of us walked the campus that night, everything Ron had worked toward for four years seemed to be gone.

   But do you know what happened to Ron? The crisis he faced with the med school got resolved. By the time that happened, however, God was leading him in a different direction. Ron shifted gears and became an attorney and went on to become one of the top lawyers in the nation at what used to be called the Department of Health, Education, and Welfare.

Ultimately he oversaw all Medicare and Medicaid legislation before it went to the White House for the president's signature. Toward the end of Ronald Reagan's presidency, exploratory negotiations were taking place for Ron to be on the White House staff.

Yes, God had a different plan for his life. But it took a crisis and an apparent defeat for God to move him from a very fine career to an incredible one.

6. **Pray more when you are faced with an ongoing crisis**. Pray early, pray late. I've prayed early now for a number of years, and I'm always a changed man by the time I get up off my knees. When it's over, I feel I've become a different person. Which, of course, is what the Bible promises and is exactly what I'm hoping for. Are you receptive to that much help, or do you just hope to get through your crisis on your own?

7. **Don't go backward after God gives you a victory**. Often a physical and emotional letdown occurs after a victory. The old prophet Elijah is a classic case in point. In 1 Kings chapter 17 Elijah bursts on the scene of a rebellious Israel that is worshiping Baal, the sun God, and has turned its back on the Creator. God wants to get their attention, not just because He's hurt. Baal worshipers didn't just worship the sun. They also sacrificed their babies to him.

Anyway, God calls on Elijah and launches him into a monumental crisis when he sends him with this message for Israel's rebellious King Ahab: *"There won't be any rain for the next several years until I say so."*

Then Elijah takes off for the woods. But he's hardly a happy camper. He stays alive by eating food brought by birds while Ahab is trying to kill him. And if this isn't enough, Elijah goes through a series of at least twelve additional crises over the next three and a half years.

For instance, He knew when he told King Ahab there would be no more rain that the king would try to kill him. After a short time he has to leave his hiding place when the creek in the woods dries up.

Third crisis: He is directed to go to a foreign country and live with a widow who has just run out of food and has a small boy to feed.

He obeys, and the Lord keeps all three in food for months. Until crisis number four occurs. The boy dies.

Not a big deal for the Lord. God uses Elijah to resurrect him.

Crisis number five takes place at the three-and-a-half-year mark when God sends Elijah back to Ahab, who, of course, hasn't given up on the idea of killing him.

When Elijah runs into Obadiah, Ahab's chief of staff, crisis number six takes place. Obadiah refuses to cooperate with Elijah. He doesn't want to lose his head.

So in crisis number seven Elijah is forced to confront Ahab in person.

Crisis 8 ensues when he confronts the 450 prophets of Baal with the entire nation of Israel looking on. A significant aspect of this is what I call Crisis 9, when Elijah calls for fire from heaven to consume the sacrifice. This sacrifice is a symbol of Jesus Christ, the Lamb of God, who will one day die for our rebellious and snakebit ways.

Crisis 10 involves Elijah overseeing the execution of 450 false prophets of Baal. Some Bible scholars believe he participated in killing them.

Crisis 11 is Elijah's prayer for rain. That was a crisis because nothing happened!

Have you ever prayed in a crisis—and nothing happened? That's what happened to Elijah. He prayed for rain—with King Ahab looking on—and nothing happened. So he prayed again. And nothing happened. And he prayed again. Nothing. And again. Nothing. Six times he prayed for rain, and six times nothing happened.

If you're a person of prayer, how many times do you repeat your requests when nothing happens?

Well, Elijah prays a seventh time, refusing to give up. Finally his servant tells the worn-out prophet that he sees a small cloud in the west. And that told Elijah that it was going to rain.

Then it's on to Crisis 12, a seventeen-mile marathon. Elijah actually runs in front of Ahab's horses, guiding them in a rainstorm over a seventeen-mile stretch to the capital city of Jezreel.

Do you know how far seventeen miles are? I ran a marathon once, and let me tell you, I was starting to feel it by the time I reached the seventeen-mile mark. At any rate, after getting the king home, Elijah throws his cloak over his head—and crashes. He desperately needs about a week of uninterrupted sleep followed by a long vacation. Instead, a few hours later, he is awakened out of what must have been the deepest sleep anyone could possibly experience only to hear a nightmare message from Queen Jezebel: *"By this time tomorrow, you'll be a dead man!"*

Elijah loses it, and who can blame him? It's an ironic twist. One minute he's running in front of Ahab's horses—a few hours later, running for his life! Elijah not only caves, he ends up *in* a cave on a mountain called Horeb.

And it's there that Elijah and God get reconnected and Elijah's unending crisis finally ends.

Do you have a crisis in your life that just won't quit? Or maybe *a series* of crises? Perhaps you're trying to trust God, but you're sure wondering where He's been lately, and you're in an emotional cave?

The answer is He's right beside you—and within you if you'll allow that. God tells you and me that if necessary He will even carry us. *"I am he who will sustain you. I have made you and I will carry you. I will sustain you and I will rescue you"* (Isaiah 46:4). *"I will never leave you nor forsake you"* (Hebrews 13:5).

Elijah came out of his crisis all right. He had a few more crises and then went to heaven, becoming one of the very few on this planet who've never died. In fact, a few hundred years later when Jesus was going through His own crisis just before the cross, Elijah had the incredible privilege of joining Moses as the two helped the King of the universe get through His worst crisis—His nightmare death on the Cross for you and me. When you get to heaven, don't forget to look up Elijah and thank him for doing that.

So if you've been going through a crisis that just won't quit, remember, God's still in charge. He still has a plan for your life. In the hour of your greatest weakness and despair when everything seems lost, keep trusting God. He will reward your faith.

8.  **Simplify your life when you're going through a major crisis**. Solomon put it this way: *"When times are good, be happy; but when times are bad, consider"* (Ecclesiastes 7:14).

    Cut back on everything when you are in crisis. Simplify your diet, your entertainment, your lifestyle. No overtime at work. You need perspective; you need wisdom. And you won't find either if you're out drinking or chowing down greasy foods. Or home watching hours of TV. You need time for reflection, hopefully prayerful reflection.

    A timeout will give you power to cope and absorb God's promises, such as, *"My grace is sufficient for you, for my power is made perfect in weakness"* (2 Corinthians 12:9). Just remember, if you don't take time to refuel, you're sure to run out of gas. Keep your life simple in times of crisis.

9.  **Prepare now for tomorrow's crises**. Our world is a battle zone between the forces of good and evil. Like Muhammad Ali, you and I must contend some days against crises that rain down against us like George Foreman's body blows and head shots. But the good news is that we never have to fight alone. And don't forget, the One who fights *with* us has also promised to fight *for* us. *"The Lord will fight for you,"* He tells us, *"you have only to be still"* (Exodus 14:14).

    Got a crisis going on in your life? Take a second look at Jesus in Revelation 1. There, with eyes like *"blazing fire"* (verse 14), His face *"like the sun shining in all its brilliance"* (verse 16), and a sharp, double-edged sword coming out of His mouth, we see a much different Jesus than most of us are used to. One look at this Jesus, and you'll have no doubt that He's the God who can get you through any crisis.

10. **Remember, as long as you trust God, a crisis can never defeat you even though you may appear to be defeated.** So your crisis isn't fixed, and you end up with a bad grade, a failed business deal, a divorce, continued pain or illness. What then? Where was God when you needed Him?

    Jesus had the same question as He hung on the Cross. Jesus on the Cross endured the greatest crisis the universe has ever seen. If

Jesus fails here, you and I are toast, and God's reputation is forever sullied throughout the universe.

So as Jesus hangs there naked and bleeding with our sins crushing out His life, He reaches out to His Father—and there is no response. Only a void.

Earlier Jesus has said, *"I and the Father are one"* (John 10:30). Now He can't find the Father.

Have you ever had a relationship go south and when you tried to find the other person, he or she just wasn't there? You reached out, but there was just a void. Now *that's* a crisis!

Multiply the pain of that kind of crisis by a few billion times (He died for all of us, after all) and maybe we can get a hint of what our sins did to Jesus on the Cross. They crushed the life out of Him. And when He was hanging there naked, panting out His life to save you and me, His mind blinded by searing pain and thoughts that He was never coming back from the grave, you'll have to agree it didn't look as if He was winning the fight.

Today, of course, we see what He did as the most magnificent victory in the universe. The lesson for you and me is simple: Whenever you're in crisis and everything appears hopeless, you can never be defeated as long as your faith in God endures.

I think of my former editorial colleague, Ken McFarland. A number of years ago when doctors told Ken his cancer was terminal and that he had six months or less to live, Ken went to his knees, made some lifestyle changes in his diet, and looked to Jesus. He's still standing today, free at this writing years later from all cancer.

Job said, *"Though He slay me, yet will I trust Him"* (Job 13:15) When you and I can say those words, we too will go from apparent defeat to victory after victory over every crisis. Why not start practicing saying those words right now?

"Though He slay me, yet will I trust Him!"

"Though He slay me, yet will I trust Him!"

"Though He slay me, yet will I trust Him!"

# CHAPTER NINE

# How to Think Straight

*"The happiness of your life depends upon the quality of your thoughts; therefore, guard them accordingly"*
—Marcus Aurelius

How do you feel about your ability to think? Feel as if you do okay—that you make pretty good decisions most of the time? Let's take a quick look at what the Bible says about our ability to think, yours included. Prepare to be perplexed.

The prophet Isaiah says, *"The whole head is sick ... there is no soundness in it"* (Isaiah 1:5, 6).

When he was 8 or 9 years old, one of my sons cut his finger while playing outside in our yard. When I didn't look at the injury as quickly as he wanted me to, he was offended. *"I hope they have to cut it off and it costs you a million dollars!"* he said. Now that wasn't really good thinking on his part, most of us would agree. But, hey, he was just a kid, right?

Okay, so let's look at the thinking of a few adults and see if their thinking is better. Do you remember (or have heard of, if you're young) Karen Carpenter, a singer from back in the 70s and 80s with a fabulous voice? Even though she was severely underweight, she died of anorexia because she experienced herself as fat even though she was a string bean.

Consider the thinking of former Los Angeles Lakers basketball player Rick Fox talking about how to win at basketball: *"When you've got a team down, you've got to* **suffocate** *them. You have to look within and* **find all the evil** *you can. I'm telling you, you have to. It's not something you want your kids hearing, but we're grown men, battling out there for the same thing.*

Think about the implications of that kind of thinking. Do any past world leaders come to mind?

Christian author Ellen White wrote that humans were *"originally endowed with noble powers and a well-balanced mind."* But when Adam and Even disobeyed God, she says, *"selfishness took the place of love,"*[1] and *"the whole human organism [became] deranged, the mind perverted, the imagination corrupted."*

Thousands of years ago in heavenly realms, selfishness and pride were unknown elements until Lucifer, the brightest mastermind in all creation, became mysteriously infected with it. The result? His self-centered thinking became so distorted that he became a god in his own eyes and thought he could dethrone the Creator. Once he actively rebelled, his thinking was never normal again.

And now for the bad news. You and I have inherited his nature! That's why the thrust of this book isn't to help you get better but rather to get replaced.

You see, apart from God, even the brightest among us can't think straight. Consider my friends Jennifer and John. Married, but not to each other, they fell madly in love. (Remember that word *madly*, because they didn't realize until later that they were out of their minds.) At the very least, they would both admit later they weren't thinking straight.

Jennifer worked for me, and when she and John told me of their intention to hook up, I said, *"How can you two possibly find lasting happiness under these circumstances? You guys will be breaking up two homes."*

But nothing could stop them. Jennifer told me, *"I have found the love of my life, and I'm not going to let this opportunity pass me by."* So they got divorces, ripped apart two families, and damaged the lives of five children. As she told me goodbye, Jennifer said, *"I promise to stay in touch. I'll let you know how we do."*

---

1.    *Steps to Christ* and *The Ministry of Healing,* by Ellen G. White.

Six months later she phoned. *"Mike, I had to let you know what's going on. I live in a beautiful home. I have everything I could ever want—and I'm going through hell."* She went on to describe how her marriage was failing and that John had recently, in her words, *"beaten me to a pulp."*

Later with her new marriage continuing to unravel, Jennifer told me that her previous husband should have had her committed to a psychiatric facility.

Jennifer and John went into counseling, but nothing helped. Within a year they were divorced, all because they couldn't think straight at a critical time in their lives.

Don't be too hard on Jennifer and John. If you and I don't have God in our lives, we can't think straight either. The Bible reminds us, *"The whole head is sick"* Isaiah 1:5. So we're likely to make some irrational decisions, too, especially if we're thinking primarily about ourselves and have the mindset that many do, *"We only go around once—let's grab all the gusto we can get."*

The Bible also tells us that not long after the fall of Adam and Eve, every inclination of man's thoughts *"was only evil all the time"* (see Genesis 6:5). When Jesus commented on human nature, He said, *"Out of the heart come evil thoughts."* Then He went on to recite an ugly list including *"murder, adultery, sexual immorality, theft, false testimony, slander"* (Matthew 15:19). Any of these you? Never had the urge to ____? No evil thoughts?

Can you see why God offers all of us *new* minds and hearts? (2 Corinthians 2:16; Ezekiel 36:26).

Several years ago a friend who is in the medical profession visited me. He didn't have God in his life at the time, and when he talked to me about his thinking processes, he described them as *"the hell going on inside my head"* as he discussed personal problems with me.

I said to him, *"Hank, let Jesus into your life."*

Do you know why he wouldn't at the time? Because he wasn't thinking straight. He told me he was afraid of what the devil would throw at him if he became a Christian. I told him, *"You don't have to worry about the devil, Hank. Jesus beat the devil a long time ago."*

But Hank said he had to run.

If you'd like to think straight, please consider the following three points along with the protocol at the end of this chapter.

1. **Be sure you are experiencing the Exchanged Life (see chapter 4).** No matter how high our IQ, the natural self we're born with has no ability to think straight. If self is alive, our thinking is always distorted. So if you haven't already done so, exchange your old self every day for the new supernatural self that God offers.

2. **Ask God to give you *"the mind of Christ."*** The only way to think straight is to permit your Creator to inhabit your brain and to give you the mind of Christ every day—something He has promised to do.[2]

   The apostle Paul underscores this point when he says, *"Let this mind be in you which was also in Christ Jesus"* (Philippians 2:5). He goes on to encourage us to be transformed by the renewing of your mind" (Romans 12:2). *"For God did not give us a spirit of timidity,"* the Bible tells us, *"but a spirit of power, of love, and of a sound mind"* (2 Timothy 1:7). Ask the Holy Spirit to give you a sound mind every day, and He will.

3. **Turn your mind away from worthless things**. We become changed by whatever we look at. The psalmist asked God, *"Turn my eyes away from worthless things"* (Psalm 119:37) and so must we. The apostle Paul recommends that we think about those things that are true, noble, right, pure, lovely, and admirable (Philippians 4:8). So don't dwell on wrong thoughts if you want your thinking to be healthy. The Bible says that even God can't bear to look upon evil (Habakkuk 1:13).

If you're someone who needs major help with your thought patterns, know that Jesus will get the job done if you will exchange your mind for His every day.

Consider sexual fantasies for a moment. Clinical psychologists claim that about 95 percent of both men and women indulge sexual fantasies. And many psychologists, researchers, and authors in this field believe such fantasies are harmless. *"You can safely fantasize about your yoga teacher without really having an affair and ruining your marriage,"* says

---

2. *"But we have the mind of Christ"* (1 Corinthians 2:15).

Karl Bauer, coauthor of the widely circulated college textbook, *Our Sexuality.* He goes on to state that people should use their fantasies as a *"way to have it all without suffering the consequences."*

They are wrong who dismiss sexual fantasies as harmless. No married person is going to enhance his or her relationship with a spouse by indulging immoral thoughts. And for single persons who pursue such thoughts—will any future relationship ever be able to compete with the intoxication of immoral fantasy thinking? Not likely!

Several years ago a male friend told me a particular sexual fantasy had such a hold on him that he doubted his life with his wife would ever be normal again. Another friend told me that his fantasizing had resulted in his actually carrying out an immoral fantasy in real life.

The Bible declares this principle: As a person *"thinks in his heart, so is he"* (Proverbs 23:7) My pastor friend, Clarence Schilt, says it well: *"What gets the mind gets us. And what gets us is reported in our thoughts, attitudes, words, and actions."*

Let me share with you briefly some science on how the mind works. Every time you think any kind of thought, a small neural pathway begins to form in your brain. If that thought is repeated, the pathway deepens. Some of us who are older probably have some pretty deep ruts in our brains! But while old thought patterns can never be completely *erased,* given enough repetitions they can be *overridden* by new thoughts. *It is actually possible to establish new neural highways atop the old negative ones in your brain.*

With this in mind, let me remind you of my personal experience I shared earlier about this business of learning to think straight. Earlier in my life, I was afflicted with thinking so flawed I can only describe it as mental illness. Let me say it again for emphasis: I was mentally ill! From my teen years forward, I'd fantasize snakebit thoughts. This continued into adulthood. I would confess these thoughts to God, get a temporary victory, and then some difficulty would come into my life, and I would try to medicate the pain with my old addiction.

As I wrote in the *"Heart of the Matter"* chapter, about fifteen years ago I told God, *"I want this addiction out of my life forever."* That was the beginning of a ferocious struggle. I felt that I'd rather die than give up this way of thinking. Finally I said to God, *"I'm asking you to kill this sickness and give me the mind of Christ. And if You can't do that, then I give You permission to kill me. Just take me out."*

I will praise God forever because He killed my illness and let me live. Yet in a sense, I did die. I died to a snakebit self and my baggage of degraded thinking. When I permitted Jesus to have 100 percent of my life, I received not only the mind of Christ, I also received a new self. A new nature. I became a different person.

*"How long did this take?"* you may wonder. I believe the change took place the moment I made this decision and offered God unrestricted access into my life. I slipped a few times after that, but even in the slippage, I detected that things were different once I made my decision. God had erected a barrier in my mind and heart that was already neutralizing my old compulsion. *But the most important thing I learned was that I needed to make this decision daily.*

On those rare occasions when I've *indulged* it (and that's been a long time now), the addiction became like falling into a terrifying and powerful current like that described in the next chapter.

Wrong thinking always gave me an incredible high. But it was a high that was always followed by a trip into an awful low. For me, that was the tradeoff—major depression in exchange for a fleeting high. Not a good deal.

God's gift to us for correct thinking is peace and contentment. And the peace He gives isn't boring. It is an animated, living pleasure that powers up all of our moral energies and equips us to make a difference in the lives of those around us instead of using them. This isn't just a *good* way to live, it's the *only* way to live!

*How long does it take to reach full wellness? Psychologists tell us it takes about a month to six weeks to really get a new habit going.* Beyond that, many feel it takes the mind about six months to reformat itself. One friend of mine, a psychologist, maintains that it can take longer to reach complete wellness.

So don't give up too quickly once you start processing the protocols from chapter 4. With every act of implementing them, you're training your 86 billion neurons (that's the newest number) to do the right thing and turn away from evil.

So don't get discouraged if you don't have instant success. The gurus on behavioral change maintain that change is a process. Put God in charge of that process every day, and He will get you where you need to be.

By the way, in the for-what-it's-worth department, I ask God every day to put enmity between me and the things of the world and the flesh. I also ask Him to give me the mind of Christ, an appetite for righteousness, and a hunger for holiness! I don't miss.

The most important point is what I call "processing." That means no matter how things are going in my life, I exchange my mind for the mind of Jesus Christ every day as I go through the protocol described in chapter 4.

When I do this, I begin *experiencing* God. I don't simply have God in mind—I have God in my mind. I also have His power. *"Look,"* He says, *"I give you power...over all the power of the enemy"* (Luke 10:19). I have God, and God has me. As I claim these promises every morning, I see myself as one of God's special-ops guys in a war zone, ready for anything.

Before I obtained the mind of Christ, I saw myself as of little value, almost worthless. Now I see myself having great value because I no longer have distorted thinking. I see myself today as royalty, which I am—*a blood-bought soul of the King of the universe.* By the way, as your thinking becomes normal, your behavior won't be far behind. Behavior always follows how we think, for better or for worse.

Let Jesus into your life right now, and you too can begin to think straight. And if you keep letting Him into your life daily, the Bible says you'll begin reflecting the glory of the Lord and be transformed into His likeness (2 Corinthians 3:18).

What if you crash and burn along the way? Well, you will. But when that happens, be encouraged by this wonderful promise: *"For though a righteous [person] falls seven times, he rises again"* (Proverbs 24:16). Look at it again and you'll note it's calling a person righteous whose behavior has been repeatedly awful. Perhaps this is weak little you. You see, God accounts you righteous long before your behavior gets there. It's a gift. Jesus still has your back, kiddo.

So don't feel defeated when you blow it. Just keep asking every day for what the Bible promises —an exchanged life, a new heart, and the mind of Christ.

*Finally, every time you find a wrong thought in your mind, resist it.* I can't tell you how important this is. *Submit yourself to God, then resist the wrong thought, asking God to replace it with one of His own. This is essential in forcing the devil to flee.* Not to resist is to allow Satan to make your mind his playground, and he never plays fair (despite the well-known Charlie Daniels song, *"The Devil Went Down to Georgia,"* stating the contrary).

So resist even when you desperately don't want to. When you do this, the Holy Spirit will enable you to *"take captive every thought to make it obedient to Christ"* (2 Corinthians 10:5). And God *"will satisfy your desires with good things"* (Psalm 103:5). That's a promise.

Often this will be a hellish battle, but the outcome is always wonderful. For the Bible promises that God always *"fulfills the desires of those who fear him"* (Psalm145:16). And that's a promise too. Be sure to claim it.

By the way, don't get down on yourself for having a wrong thought. Apparently the devil is able to plant snakebit thoughts in our minds. Having a wrong thought is not a sin. Indulging it is.

So as you begin each new day, experiment with the seven-point protocol which comes next and watch what happens.

## A Healing-for-Your-Mind Protocol

1. **Invite God into your life every morning before you do anything else.** Jesus says in the Bible, *"I stand at the door and knock. If anyone opens the door, I will come in"* (Revelation 3:20). So tell Him, *"Jesus, please come in. I choose to give You unrestricted access into my life and to surrender my will to Your will. I acknowledge I am a blood-bought soul of the King of the universe."*

2. **Ask God to give you a new heart and to install His mind in place of your mind.** Just say, *"Lord, You've promised to give me a new heart and have said that if I've received You, I can have Your mind. Please give me these two gifts today through your indwelling Holy Spirit."* (Ezekiel 36:26; 1 Corinthians 2:16).

3. **Ask Jesus to evict any powers of darkness that might be in your life and light up your life with the Holy Spirit.** *"Not by power nor by might, but by My Spirit, says the Lord"* (Zechariah 4:6).

4. **Invite Jesus to change you into a different person.** Just tell Him, "Lord, you told Saul in the Old Testament, *'The Spirit of the Lord will come upon you with power...and you will be changed into a different person.'* (1 Samuel 10:6*). Please change me into a different person, too*."

5. **Practice "eating" God's Bible promises.** The prophet Jeremiah once wrote, *"When Your words came, I ate them. They were my joy and my heart's delight"* (Jeremiah 15:16). **For example, here's how you can "eat" (receive) promises such as the following**: Just say, "Lord, You've said, *'For God did not give [me] a spirit of fear, but a spirit of power, and of love, and of a sound mind'* (2 Timothy 1:7). I claim this promise in Jesus' name."

   Here are some additional promises you might practice claiming (receiving into your mind):

   **If you're tempted to fight**: *"The Lord will fight for you, and you have only to be still"* (Exodus 14:14).

   **When you're unsure what to do**: *"I will teach you and instruct you in the way you should go"* (Psalm 32:8).

   **When you're feeling lonely:** *"I will never leave you nor forsake you"* (Hebrews 13:5).

   **Why "eating" God's Word is a good idea:** *"The word of God is full of living power"* (Hebrews 4:12).

   **When you're feeling empty:** *"God has given us the Holy Spirit to fill our hearts with His love"* (Romans 5:5).

   **If you're tempted to use:** *"Don't get drunk.... Instead, be filled with the Spirit"* (Ephesians 5:18).

   **When you're anxious or dissatisfied:** *"Don't be afraid. I am your shield and your exceeding great reward"* (Genesis 15:1).

6. **Every morning thank God for one to five things.** For starters, since 153,000 die worldwide every day, why not thank God for

another day of life? Choosing to have an attitude of gratitude will bring healing to your mind and body.

7. **Do something nice for someone today** (that's what you're here for). This can be as simple as saying hi to a stranger and smiling.

Process each of these points for seven straight days, and you'll start to think straighter as God changes you into an exciting new person and floods your mind and heart with His love.

# CHAPTER TEN

# The Day the River Tried to Kill Me

On June 30, 2011, as my son Pat and I floated Central Oregon's beautiful John Day River, I had no idea my life would become a nightmare and almost end when I was suddenly catapulted into wild whitewater and trapped in an icy current that wouldn't let me go.

The John Day drains the Strawberry Mountains of Central Oregon and meanders for 284 miles before it empties into the mighty Columbia River. It's a pretty little river—the second-longest free-flowing river in the United States. My wife, Diane, and I had floated the John Day many times before without incident in our two-person raft. I had no idea the river had the heart of a dragon and might try to kill me one day.

Scott Field, owner of an RV camp in the little town of Spray (population 500), wasn't on hand when Pat and I arrived. If he had been, I might have learned that a late spring had kept the river's temperature unusually cold for this time of year—only 40 degrees. A search-and-rescue person in the area told me a week later, *"Ten minutes in water that cold, and you'd have been dead."*

Later, Pat and I calculated I was in the river close to eight minutes. If Scott had been around, I might also have learned that someone drowns in the John Day every two to three years.

It was a gloomy day, raining heavily, when Pat and I set off from my home in Gresham. Pat is one of my three sons and is a policeman living in Texas. An hour down the road we left the Columbia Gorge and entered the high-desert country of Central Oregon, the rain ended, and the day became blue-sky beautiful. Miles of grain fields punctuated with undulating windmills dotted the landscape.

At the outset, Pat and I faced a three-and-a-half-hour drive from Gresham to Spray, where we would begin our float trip. By the time we arrived, the landscape had changed from sweeping grain fields to forests and spectacular rock formations, with mountains rising upward to 1,000 feet or more in places.

It was a wowzer of a day, sunny with temperatures in the mid 80s, when Pat and I had prayer and started out. A little past noon, we shoved off. I was at the oars while Pat fished. The current didn't seem overly strong as we started down the river. I had no idea what loomed ahead.

For the next three hours our float went smoothly. We ran a few rapids and looked for some good holes for Pat to fish. We had great conversation and were enjoying the spectacular beauty all around us. Of course we had our life vests on.

Later that night when he couldn't sleep, Pat recorded his memory of our accident. In his own words, *"As we went along, we passed through several areas of white water without incident. When Dad told me to get low, I would, and we went through the rapids just fine. However, after about three hours, we began to approach the area where Dad had left the car. At the same time, we neared another set of rapids that looked far more intense than any previous white water. These rapids looked high and deep. I got low in the raft and prepared myself. However, nothing could prepare me for what would happen next.*

*"Dad suddenly got thrown from the raft and into the white water. I didn't see him go in—I heard him go in. I turned around in time to see him come up out of the water gasping for breath.*

*Dad's launch into the water seemed to push me and the raft into calmer water near the bank. But in seconds, Dad's body was ripped away by the powerful current before I could reach him. I had him in sight one minute, only to watch him disappear beneath the white water as the current pulled him under again and again."*

When the river struck, it struck with fury. One minute I was in the raft in 83-degree sunshine trying to maneuver to shore, the next in a raging torrent of frigid, 40-degree white water trying to kill me. I was helpless in the maelstrom. I would barely make it to the surface, gasp, spit water, and immediately get dragged under, my life vest helpless to keep me afloat.

Words are inadequate to describe the violence of the rapids and the power of the current. As the river tried to drown me, I remember praying once during my nightmare, *"Dear Jesus, please. Not here—not now!"* My 72-year-old body began weakening rapidly after being sucked under at least four times as it was dish-ragged through nearly 100 yards of white water. Horror swept over me. I felt sure I was going to die.

One aspect of my survival was that my body never got smashed on the many rocks in the white water. That was miraculous in itself. In previous floats, Diane's and my little raft often crashed against the rocks when we went through white water. Thankfully, that didn't happen to me.

A quarter of a mile downstream and perhaps a minute or two later, I was finally out of the white water. But a powerful current took me to the middle of the river, never allowing my stricken body anywhere near one of the banks I so desperately needed to find. After five or six minutes in these conditions, my efforts to swim were becoming very feeble as my body began shutting down. I was barely able to move.

In the meantime, Pat got our raft to the bank and clambered out. Later that night he recorded these thoughts: *"We were in the middle of nowhere with no cell phone service. I knew that for my Dad to survive, he would somehow have to get himself to shore.*

*"My background in police work has given me opportunities to work through some difficult situations. But I've never been as afraid as I was now. If he died, what would I tell Diane, his wife? What would I tell my two brothers? As I scrambled up the embankment, I could feel tears coming to my eyes. And I prayed again and again, 'Please, God, save my dad,' as I ran down the road to look for him."*

Just as I was about to give up, a river bank suddenly appeared a few feet in front of me and along with it some small bushes. I gave a desperate lunge and grabbed a handful. Then I just lay in the rushing water for a few moments parallel to the bank, unable to move as the river tried to take me back. But I knew that somehow I had to get out. So slowly, inch by inch, face-down in the mud, I began to drag my benumbed body out of the river.

Here is Pat's description of how he found me:

*"I ran down the road until I came to a dirt road that led toward the river where I had last seen my dad. I began calling for him, but there was no reply, and my heart sank.*

*"I ran further down the road to a second area. Still no sign of him.*

*"As I ran toward a third area close to a half mile from where he'd fallen in, I knew if I couldn't find him now, it would be too late. I called out to him, but there was no answer. Then suddenly I spotted him about thirty feet below. As I climbed down the rocks, I could see he was covered from head to foot with mud and sand.*

*"I was relieved to see him, but that changed when I drew close. His skin was pasty white, his breathing short and labored, and he wasn't able to focus or speak. I tried several times to get him to speak, but he just couldn't do it.*

*"He continued to be nonresponsive, and it was clear to me that he was in shock and needed medical attention as quickly as possible.*

*"I got the car keys out of his pocket and told him I would be back soon. I climbed back up the rocky embankment and ran the half mile to the car. When I returned, Dad's skin was still very white, his respirations shallow, and he displayed minimal cognitive function.*

*"He had lost his water sox during his ordeal, so I cleaned the mud off his feet and put dry tennis shoes on him. I told him, 'Dad, somehow we're going to have to climb up these rocks. You're going to have to give me everything you've got.'"*

As Pat tried to get me up to the car, I was like a boxer who had just been knocked out. Picture me with my right arm around Pat's neck and Pat's arm around my waist, the two of us slowly picking our way around huge rocks up the steep twenty-five to thirty-foot embankment toward the car.

No doubt if anyone had seen us, they would have thought, *"Those guys have had too much to drink."* Actually I was dehydrated as well as exhausted.

At last I made it to the top and collapsed into the car as Pat drove us about five miles back to Spray to seek help. However, there were no medics around, and I had a major headache. So I asked Pat to buy me some aspirin at one of the two general stores.

I got two aspirin down with the help of some bottled water, and we began the thirty-three-mile drive to the little town of Fossil where there was a small medical facility. More than forty-five minutes out of the river on a very warm day in Central Oregon, my temperature was still only 96.8 rather than the normal 98.6. I can only imagine how cold my hypothermic body must have been when I first crawled out of the river.

My ordeal on the John Day River was finally over. My gracious God enabled me to get out of a current that was trying to kill me. As you'd expect, I'm grateful to still be here. And a smile comes to my face whenever I read Isaiah 43:2-4: *"When you pass through the waters, I'll be with you; and through the rivers, they will not [drown] you, for I am the Lord Your God.... Your Savior...and I love you"* (Isaiah 43:2-4).

Ever find yourself in a current that's killing you? It doesn't have to be a river. Perhaps yours is a current of doubt, of an addiction, of unforgiveness, of a snakebit mind. Or maybe it's an unhappy relationship or negative thinking. If you're caught in a bad current just now, calling out to God for help may well be the most important first step you can take.

After all, He has promised, *"Call to Me and I will answer you"* (Jeremiah 33:3).

# CHAPTER ELEVEN

# How to Become a Happier Camper

How happy are you? And by happy, I am talking about feeling contented, blessed, joyful.

However you answer, you'll be interested to know that science has now discovered that our level of happiness comes packaged in our genes. That's right, we all have a happiness default level where we live most of the time. What's cool about this new information is that if you're unhappy, you now have tools with which to boost your level of happiness. This chapter will help you learn how.

So how happy are you? Not sure? Then take the *Happiness Quiz*[1] that follows and find out. Then you can decide what to do next.

For each item below, select a number from 0 to 6 and write it next to the statement. Zero means you disagree totally; 3 means you're not sure; and 6 means you agree totally:

___ My life is very close to my ideal.

___ The conditions of my life are excellent.

___ I am completely satisfied with my life.

___ So far, I have obtained the important things I want in my life.

___ If I could live my life over, I would change nothing.

---

1.  *The Happiness Quiz* was created by Ed Diener, Ph.D., professor of psychology at the University of Illinois at Urbana–Champaign.

___ Total Score

How happy are you? Here is the scorecard:

    26-30 = Extremely happy

    21-25 = Very happy

    15-20 = Somewhat happy

    11-14 = Somewhat unhappy

    6-10 = Very unhappy

    0-5 = Extremely unhappy

So did you have a pretty good fix on how happy you are? If you came in about where you thought you would, that means you know yourself pretty well—and that should make you happy![2]

How happy do you think the people around you are? Your friends, classmates, colleagues at work? Demographic researchers tell us that most aren't overly happy and that many suffer from depression.

Even though our quality of life in the West has risen significantly since World War II, the number of people who consider themselves happy has remained flat for the last fifty years. In fact, researchers tell us that people today are ten times *more* likely to suffer from depression than those born two generations ago.[3]

What does it take to make you happy? A decent job? Enough money to pay the bills? A week in the Bahamas? A vacation in Disneyland? Good health, landing a thirty-pound king salmon, a good relationship, a meal with friends, a piece of moist chocolate cake? What works for you?

Making enough money to pay the bills doesn't necessarily make for happiness. Neither does intelligence, prestige, or sunny weather. According to researchers, good looks help but only marginally. And alcohol works, but only until the buzz wears off. After that, it's depression time.

Those who research such matters tell us that a strong marriage, family

---

2.    Though the Happiness Quiz is helpful, most of its questions focus on either the present or the past. Some may find that if they focus more fully on the future—factoring in their hopes, optimism, and even expectations—their happiness score will be considerably higher.

3.    *U.S. News & World Report*, September 3, 2001.

ties, friendships, spirituality, and a healthy self-esteem play a powerful role in determining how happy we are. They also say that having hope is critical, along with the feeling that life has meaning. Do you feel that your life has meaning? How much hope do you have?

Do you remember the comedian Rodney Dangerfield? Rodney developed a very successful show-business career from the line, *"I don't get no respect!"* Well, it turns out that despite his successful career, Rodney wasn't a very happy guy. In fact, you might be surprised at what he said about his state of happiness to an interviewer several years ago. *"I've never been happy,"* Dangerfield said. *"My whole life has been a downer."*

The interviewer was shocked. He said he'd done hundreds of celebrity interviews and had never been more uncomfortable than he was with this one. Stunned, he tried to soothe Dangerfield's hurt. He said that surely the comedian must have been happy at some point in his life—perhaps as a child. To which the comedian responded, *"There was nothing about my childhood that made me happy, and the scars of youth stay with you forever."*

He went on to explain that he was reared by his mother after his parents separated. *"We lived in a neighborhood that was too rich for us. Every day after school I would deliver food to the back doors of the homes where the rich kids lived. It was humiliating and made me want to escape. They say people go into show business for the recognition, and maybe that's why I went into it. I know I never got any recognition from my mother or father."*

During the interview, the writer suggested that the love of millions of fans must surely be some consolation. To which Dangerfield replied, *"The people don't love me. They love my work. And even if they do love me, it's not enough to make me happy."*

So we see that even a successful career and wealth aren't enough to bring happiness. If success, money, intelligence, a good education, physical attractiveness, and having nice things don't bring all that much happiness, what does?

If you aren't very happy, here are six points to help you raise your happiness level.

**Take time to appreciate the little things.** Little things really are the stuff of happiness *if* we take the time to notice them. But if the TV is always on or we're on the run most of the time, we miss out. Turn the darn TV off. Take time to enjoy the little things—a flower budding, a moon rising, a rainbow, the happy laughter of a child.

**Practice being grateful**. Being grateful is huge! Robert Emmons of the University of California–Davis found that people who wrote down five things for which they were grateful in a weekly or daily journal were not only happier, they also were healthier, less stressed, more optimistic, and more likely to help others.[4]

You might give this a try. It takes most people less than a minute to come up with five things for which they are grateful.

Along the same line, University of Miami psychology professor Michael McCullough found that habitually expressing gratitude also makes people happier. Subjects who wrote in a daily "gratitude journal" improved their sense of well-being in just a few weeks.

In my personal devotional life, I find that praising God improves my happiness level. Here's one example of how I do that. I often express praise to God through Scripture, such as Psalm 103:1-3. Specifically, I pray out loud and say to the Lord, *"In the words of the psalmist, I also would like to say . . ."* And then I pray the words of this psalm. Perhaps you'll experiment with it, too, and then notice the effect it has on your mood.

> *"Bless the Lord, O my soul, and all that is within me, bless His holy name.*
>
> *Bless the Lord, O my soul, and forget not His benefits.*
>
> *Who forgives all your iniquity;*
>
> *Who heals all your diseases;*
>
> *Who redeems your life from the pit;*
>
> *Who crowns you with steadfast love and mercy;*
>
> *Who satisfies you with good for as long as you live*
>
> *so that your youth is renewed like the eagles;*
>
> *Bless the Lord, O my soul"* (Psalm 103:1-3).

---

4.    Ibid.

**Learn the value of** *flow.* By *flow,* psychologists are talking about the single-minded focus of athletes and artists or anyone doing anything that poses a challenge or demands full attention. People who get into a flow are often too busy to think about happiness, but afterward they recall the experience as being incredibly positive.

Perhaps I can illustrate with my daily two-and-a-half-mile run on a treadmill at a nearby fitness center. The first few minutes are often quite painful with my arthritic knees and back. In truth, I never want to go. And on some days I'm sure I *can't* do it. But once I get into the flow, usually somewhere around the five-minute mark, it gets a lot easier, and I have a delightful sense of accomplishment afterward.

Social psychologist Susan Perry says, *"You're not jumping for joy when you're in flow, but if you are fully engaged and doing something for its own sake, that's a happy state to be in."*

Practice getting into flow on something this week (it doesn't have to be an athletic endeavor). Then evaluate your state of happiness afterward. You'll be pleased, perhaps delighted, if you really get into flow—even if it's housecleaning. (I'm allowed to say this because I do the housecleaning these days at my house, including toilets.)

**Learn to endure the bad moments without caving in**. This may sound like a strange recipe for happiness. But the Bible tells us that getting through hard moments really brings happiness. The book of James, for instance, tells us, *"Indeed, we count them blessed [happy] who endure"* (James 5:11).

Boxing trainer Teddy Atlas tells of training young Mike Tyson long before he became the heavyweight boxing champ. When Tyson was just a teenager, he was struggling to hang on in a match he was winning if he could finish. After the second round of a three-round fight, Tyson came back to his corner and said, *"I can't go on."*

Teddy told him, *"I thought you had this dream of being heavyweight champion. Let me tell you something. This is your heavyweight title fight."* Then he shoved him back out for the final round.

With about twenty seconds to go in a fight Tyson had won if he could finish the round, his opponent started pounding on him in a corner. Teddy said he could see in Tyson's eyes he was about to quit if something didn't happen. So he hopped up on the apron of the ring and bellowed almost in Tyson's ear, *"Don't do it. Don't you do it."*

Somehow Tyson hung on and won the match.

Enduring the tough moments. Not caving in. Not giving up. We all need to learn these lessons. We all face moments when we don't want to keep going, when we want to give up. But the reward for enduring those terrible moments is an almost delicious sense of happiness.

Storms never last. The times when Satan tries to overwhelm us often last only for moments. Unlike those in boxing matches, we are not alone in these struggles. Like Paul, we can declare, *"I can do all things through Him who strengthens me"* (Philippians 4:19), and God will make it so.

We can endure the worst of times and come out happy winners if we'll keep in mind in the midst of the battle such promises as these: *"And my God will supply every need of yours, according to His riches in glory in Christ Jesus"* (Philippians 4:19) and *"The Lord will fight for you, and you have only to be still"* (Exodus 14:14).

**Focus on the vertical if you want to be happy**. Most people get sucked in by the horizontal. We get out of balance and go sideways when we don't look up. Diane has a long-time friend who is chronically unhappy. She is totally focused on herself and on the horizontal. She resists Diane's attempts to point her to the vertical—toward God—and prefers to talk about suicide or about committing herself to a mental institution.

Focusing on the horizontal can drive us crazy. When I first started writing this book, the horizontal told me that I had significant health issues, a large tax bill I couldn't pay, and concern over a son who was departing for a year in Afghanistan, leaving behind a wife and two young daughters.

Just two years ago the horizontal reminded me that Diane and I might have to sell our home and downsize, that a family member who had refused to quit smoking might have a life-threatening illness, and that our beautiful view of a tree nursery with Mount Hood as a backdrop might soon be lost to a housing development.

I can go crazy if I focus on the horizontal. (By the way, many months have passed since I wrote the preceding sentences, and none of those things has occurred. Even my son who went to Afghanistan has now returned safely.)

So what does focusing on the vertical do for me? It tells me that I'm in a war but that God's in charge and that's enough.

Focusing on the vertical tells me that I've been saved for eternity through the blood of Jesus Christ, who died for my sins and who calls me one of His friends. Focusing on the vertical tells me that I don't need to sweat the small stuff—and everything is "small stuff" as long as I'm friends with Jesus.

Focusing on the vertical reminds me that someday I will sit with Jesus on His throne (see Revelation 3:21), assisting Him in the administration of the universe.[5] In light of all that lies ahead, the horizontal doesn't really matter all that much when you stop to think about it—not even if we die.

So be happy! Focus on the vertical and let the Lord take care of the horizontal. He's up to it.

**Invite God into your life every day *before* you do anything else, and you will be a much happier person.** Jesus said, Seek *first* the kingdom of God and His righteousness and your basic needs will be taken care of. (See Matthew 6:33.)

Your first inclination may be to say, *"Yeah, yeah, okay, I agree."* But how many of us really do this *before* we do anything else? I've learned that one of the dumbest things I can do when I get up in the morning is to start looking at the newspaper or turn on the TV for the weather report before I get reconnected with the Lord.

I'd like to suggest to you that in this matter, processing is everything. And when we don't process—don't do our "reps," to use a sports term—we lose out and live in the shallows instead of in the deep riches of God.

"'Lord-please-come-into-my-life-and-help-me-to-have-a-good-day'—and I'm out the door" simply doesn't cut it if I want real joy and happiness in my life.

---

5.    *"He will put him in charge of all his possessions"* (Luke 12:44).

Here are two promises that should make anyone happy. Why not ask God to make them efficacious in your life today?

*"Taste and see that the Lord is good"* (Psalm 34:8).

*"Delight yourself in the Lord and He will give you the desires of your heart"* (Psalm 37:4).

# CHAPTER TWELVE

# Do You Really Know God?

## (Or do you just know about Him?)

A Christian mentor helped me understand the difference between knowing God and just believing in Him. He told me, *"Mike, Jesus died for our sins, but it's up to you and me to die to our sinful nature."* And doing this daily is essential, because if my snakebit self is alive, it takes up all the space within me.

In other words, there's really no room for God if I'm full of myself. I may know a lot about God, but really knowing (experiencing) Him will elude me as long as my old nature has life. Below and on the following page is how the Bible describes some of the characteristics of the old and new natures in Galatians 5:19-23 and elsewhere.[1]

| Snakebit Nature | Divine Nature |
|---|---|
| Sexual Immorality | Divine Love |
| Impure Thoughts | Joy |
| Lustful Pleasure | Peace |
| Idolatry (Self-worship) | Patience |
| Demonic Activities | Kindness |

---

1.   Isaiah 1:5, 6; Jeremiah 17:9.

| | |
|---|---|
| Hostility | Goodness |
| Quarreling and Jealousy | Faithfulness |
| Outbursts of Anger | Gentleness |
| Selfish Ambition | Self-Control |
| Divisions and Envy | Power |
| Wild Parties | Healing |
| Lying/Deceitful | Truthful |

What's exciting about obtaining a new self is watching the fruit of the old self fall away and be replaced by the fruit of the new self.

I'll own up to one of the more-than-several that were mine from the *Snakebit Nature* list. That would be the *Selfish Ambition* category, easily understood when I tell you that at age 26 I had the temerity to tell the president of my company, *"I want your job."* Fortunately for me, he was gracious and encouraged me to go for it, stating that he wouldn't be around forever.

My family enjoyed me a lot more when at the age of 30 I made a Christian commitment and received a new nature. One result of doing that? I stopped working nights at the office and on weekends and became more of a father and husband.

One of the *New Nature* characteristics I took on included increased patience. I also found I was having more fulfillment in my life interacting with my three boys and wife versus climbing the corporate ladder. What a concept!

Keep in mind that I had to learn to die every day to the driven guy I had been from birth. *Selfish Ambition* was the first to go and *Idolatry* soon followed. You see, I worshiped a lot of counterfeit gods when I was younger. A counterfeit god is something that if you don't have it, you feel as if your life wouldn't have much meaning. The truth is that counterfeit gods may provide an initial rush, but they always let us down in the end.

*Do you have any counterfeit gods in your life?* A lot of people worship money, sports, cars, sex, pornography, or career success. The possibilities are endless. If you're curious about this, what you think about when you're day-dreaming might help you identify any likely suspects.

By the way, it's love of money (not money itself) that the Bible says is the root of all evil (1 Timothy 6:10). *And don't we all know folks who are in love with themselves? As I've said before, perhaps the ultimate false god is me!* Although on occasion you'll hear of someone who knowingly worships demons in exchange for money and worldly success, thus giving up on the possibility of eternal life.[2]

I still worshiped some of my counterfeit gods until about fifteen years ago (and some still try to make comebacks). That's when I had another epiphany that freed me from my devastating addiction and from two counterfeit gods I used to worship. Here's how the apostle Paul describes the process I was implementing daily:

> *"Put off your old [snakebit] self which is being corrupted by its deceitful desires…and put on the new self created to be like God in true righteousness and holiness"* (Ephesians 4:22-24).

Paul also emphasizes that the process has to be daily. *"I die daily,"* he wrote. *"I really mean that"* (1 Corinthians 15:31).

Ah, but how does one die daily? And how long does this dying business take? I don't know for sure, but I have this sense that it takes me between five and eight minutes every morning to die—to die completely the emptied-of-self kind of death. Now the truth is I really don't know if the Holy Spirit gets this done in a few seconds or a few minutes. But my sense is that I'm a very different guy after processing the protocols in chapter 4.

Does my old self come back during the night? I'm not sure. However, I do know my old self is always trying to make a comeback, and I don't want to take any chances. As I've already noted, if I'm full of myself, I won't have room for Jesus. And I certainly won't have room for you, no matter how important you should be in my life.

*Here's how this works for me. Basically, I've learned it's essential for me to become a different person every day through a supernatural encounter with God.* Before dawn, I have an interaction with the Creator-God and ask Him to change me into a nicer, kinder, more patient person. *I do this by claiming Bible promises such as these you're about to see and asking the Holy Spirit to make them a reality in my life.*

---

2. I referenced Roger Morneau's *Trip Into the Supernatural* in chapter 6, *"The Devil Made Me Do It,"* as one example of literal demon worship.

*You may find it helpful to review the protocols in chapter 4. I follow them every day, but here are five exciting promises from chapter 4 I've placed here.*

## Some Exchanged-Life Promises

*"The Holy Spirit will come upon you in power...and you will be changed into a different person"* (1 Samuel 10:6).

*"Don't copy the behavior and customs of this world, but let God transform you into a new person by changing the way you think"* (Romans 12:2).

*"I've been crucified with Christ; **it is no longer I who live, but Christ who lives in me.** And the life I now live in the flesh, I live by faith in the Son of God who loved me and gave Himself for me"* (Galatians 2:20).

*"What counts is whether we've been changed into new and different people"* (Galatians 6:15).

*"If anyone is in Christ, he is a new creation; the old has gone, the new has come"* (2 Corinthians 5:17).[3]

---

3. If I'm a new creation in Christ, why do I so often want to do the wrong thing? When you're "in Christ," you have new software—the mind of Christ. However, your hardware (your body and brain) will retain some of its old snakebit tendencies even while your software reprograms it. You'll do better as you implement your protocols, but total freedom from the old won't happen until Jesus returns, hopefully soon, and you get your new body and brain.

# CHAPTER THIRTEEN

# Me Beat Depression? Yes—You Can!

Let's say you're paralyzed by depression, barely able to think. But maybe you're able to do just one thing to get better. If so, do this:

STEP ONE. In the Bible, Jesus Christ says, *"I stand at the door and knock. If anyone opens the door, I will come in..."* (Revelation 3:20). Tell Jesus, **"Come in. You're welcome here!"**

Not sure about who Jesus is? That's okay. He says, *"Taste and see that the Lord is good"* (Psalm 34:8). Here's your chance to do exactly that.

Let Him into your life, and you'll have just done something huge. This is the Creator of the universe you've welcomed. *When you say, "Come in,"* He will, and the sunshine of His presence will beat back your darkness. You don't have to do anything else. The Bible puts it this way: *"This is the secret: Christ lives in you"* (Colossians 1:27). Imagine that! Seriously, imagine that! You can really have this experience.

What happens next is likely to be somewhat mysterious. But you'll know it's real when your darkness lifts and gets replaced by an amazing peace and joy. Don't try to explain this. Just enjoy it and know that you're experiencing what Jesus does best—bringing healing and regeneration to those who invite Him into their lives.

So enjoy the moment! And whenever the darkness tries to overtake you (the devil will try to drag you back down), simply repeat Step One and welcome Jesus anew. Each time, you'll get stronger. Your depression will weaken, and your life will be infused with joy. Keep in mind, Step One is an experience that can be repeated as often as necessary. You can't wear God out!

## What to Do Next

When you're feeling ready for a Step Two, do this: *Start **eating** some of God's promises.* The prophet Jeremiah once wrote, *"When your words came, I ate them; they were my joy and my heart's delight"* (Jeremiah 15:16). You can do the same thing. **Simply read the following promise; then claim it in Jesus' name as your own.** When you do this, the Holy Spirit will make this promise a reality in your life. I'm going to bold face it for you.

*"**The Lord is close to the brokenhearted; He rescues those who are crushed in spirit.... Taste and see that the Lord is good. Oh, the joys of those who trust in Him"*** (Psalm 34:18, 8).

*Go ahead and eat (claim, ingest) this incredible promise.* After all, Jesus has promised, *"Whatever you ask in My name, I will do it that the Father may be glorified in the Son. If you ask anything in My name, I'll do it"* (John 14:13, 14). This promise is yours to be claimed. Claim it!

*P.S.: Even if you don't feel different immediately, having claimed the promise, you'll start getting some joy in your life.* The Bible says of itself that *"the word of God is full of living power"* (Hebrews 4:12). There's only one way to find out. Check it out!

When you're ready—and there's no need to rush—go back to chapter 4 and follow the instructions in the protocol there. After that—and not until you're ready—start reading some of this additional material on depression. When you feel ready, start reading what follows here. Take your time.

## You Really Can Defeat Depression

If you suffer from depression, I believe you'll find the following story encouraging. The writer is a clinical psychologist named Doug Bloch, from Portland, Oregon, and this is his story.[1]

*In the fall of 1996, a painful divorce, a bad case of writer's block, and an*

---

1.    *Psychology Today,* December, 2000.

*adverse reaction to an antidepressant medication hurled me into a major depression. For the next ten months, I was assailed by out-of-control anxiety attacks that alternated with suicidal thoughts. Each day felt like a painful eternity."*

Bloch went on to note that his depression was deemed treatment-resistant. Antidepressants simply did not work for him. Prozac, Paxil, and Zoloft just made him agitated. Lithium made him even more depressed, and he began contemplating suicide once again. He said he felt as if he were trapped in a dark tunnel with both ends labeled "No Exit."

I'll share the rest of his story later in this chapter, but first I want to point out that if you suffer from depression, you have a lot of company. Depression cuts across all age and economic groups and includes children. One in every five persons in America is depressed, and women are twice as prone as men to be affected.

Depression currently costs American society an estimated $40 billion per year in lost work and healthcare expenses. At its worst, it simply shuts people down. It also can lead to suicide.

Some authorities call depression the world's number one public health problem—the common cold of mental illnesses. In this chapter, I will attempt to give you some tools to use if you suffer from depression—or to share if you know someone who does.

The behavioral-science profession defines depression as a mood disorder consisting of emotional dejection, with persistent feelings of sadness, anxiety, or emptiness. Depression affects the way we think and feel about ourselves and the world around us; it affects how we eat and sleep.

Other feelings associated with depression can include a sense of hopelessness, low self-esteem, feeling blue or unhappy, suffering from guilt or shame, having difficulty making decisions, feeling worthless or inadequate, or feeling paralyzed and unable to function. Am I describing any of your symptoms yet?

I would like to suggest that a major cause of depression lies in the condition of the world around us. Society teems with illness, violence, selfishness, crime, failed relationships, and death. You can't drive around any city very long without discovering a cemetery—a grim reminder of the depressing fact that no one gets out of here alive.

Statisticians tell us that in the last century alone, 231 million people around the world didn't die a normal death. They were either killed or murdered. If neither of these fates happens to us, we still must contemplate what likely *will* get us—a heart attack, cancer, stroke, diabetes, or old age. It's not a pretty picture. Indeed, observing the world around us is cause enough to bring on depression.

However, psychiatrists and psychologists tell us another primary cause of depression has to do with how we think. Distorted thinking, these folks tell us, is a major cause of depression. Simply put, the depressed person tends to think in negative and inaccurate ways about his or her life, environment, and future.

For instance, when a nondepressed person does something stupid, he or she says, *"That was stupid,"* focusing on the behavior. But the depressed person is likely to say, *"I'm such a stupid person. I can't do anything right"*—pointing toward himself. Do you see the difference?

Generally our moods are created by our thoughts. The thoughts we think at any given moment generate an immediate emotional response within us. The thought creates the emotion. For instance, a depressed person might start reading this chapter and think, *"I don't know why I'm wasting my time on this stuff."* And a negative mood will be generated. A nondepressed person might pick up this book and think, *"I'll bet I find a few nuggets here that will really be helpful."* And a more positive mood will be generated.

Now it's important to note that depression can have root causes other than from our thoughts or spiritual issues. So if the suggestions in this chapter don't work for you, please schedule an appointment with your physician. You need to learn if a physical problem is causing your depression.

In recent years, the medical profession has tended to treat depression primarily with antidepressant drugs. Some who are depressed try to treat their depression with food, sex, drugs, alcohol, etc. But these choices often get us into trouble—either because they don't work over the long haul or because we become addicted to them.

I'll never forget one of the first times I used alcohol and learned why society calls a certain time of day *Happy Hour*. Only later as I continued experimenting with alcohol did I learn about the pain and depression my increasing use brought on. I finally stopped drinking after discovering the Exchanged Life.

## Cognitive Therapy

In recent years, behavioral science professionals have discovered an alternative to drugs for treating depression. It's called cognitive therapy, and it gets results by changing the way we think. If you suffer from depression, here is a spiritually therapeutic cognitive therapy tool that I challenge you to experiment with for a victory over depression:

*The following Bible texts are intended to provide a kind of spiritual cognitive therapy for you. Claim them every day and watch these assurances from your Creator damage your depression. Receive them joyfully and get some joy in your life!*

1.  **God says He loves you**. He says, *"I've loved you with an everlasting love; with loving kindness have I drawn you"* (Jeremiah 31:3). When someone says, *"I love you,"* doesn't that generate a sweet feeling? How wonderful when those words come directly from the heart of your Creator, telling you the same thing.

2.  **The Son of God died in your place so you could live forever**. The Bible says, *"He himself bore our sins in his body on the tree, so that we might die to sin and live to righteousness; by his wounds you have been healed"* (1 Peter 2:24). We've all sinned, fallen short, and are doomed to die—which is pretty depressing. But it's wonderful to know that no matter how badly things in your life may be going just now, your Creator thinks you're valuable enough to die for.

3.  **God says He has a beautiful plan for your life**. *"'I know the plans that I have for you,' declares the Lord, 'plans to prosper you and not to cause you harm, plans to give you hope and a future'"* (Jeremiah 29:11). I try to claim that promise daily and believe it even when I can't see much happening.

4.  **God wants to give you the desires of your heart**. *"Delight yourself in the LORD and he will give you the desires of your heart"* (Psalm 37:4). Now that's a depression-beating promise. Claim it in Jesus' name.

5. **God asks you to give Him your heart so He can give you a new one**. So do that! He says, *"I'll give you a new heart and put a new spirit within you; I will take away your heart of stone and give you a heart of flesh"* (Ezekiel 36:26). Keep in mind, this needs to be a daily experience.

6. **Invite Jesus into your life.** The apostle Paul says, *"If you confess with your mouth, 'Jesus is Lord,' and believe in your heart that God raised him from the dead, you will be saved'"* (Romans 10:9). Isn't that promise a depression buster?

7. **Now start thinking correctly by receiving the mind of Christ**. The Bible says, *"Let this mind be in you which was in also in Christ Jesus"* (Philippians 2:5). As you daily open up your life anew to God, you will be *"transformed by the renewing of your mind"* (Romans 12:2). You'll start thinking correctly.

8. **With the mind of Christ, start resisting all negative and distorted thoughts.** *"Take captive every thought to make it obedient to Christ"* (2 Corinthians 10:5). At the beginning of each day, say out loud, *"In the name of Jesus Christ, I am choosing to think positive, upbeat thoughts today."* **Say these words again**. The importance of speaking our thoughts out loud is that our minds respond accordingly. Within thirty to sixty days of consistently following this practice, your thinking should change and your victories over depression become more constant.

9. **Look to Jesus in your mind daily**. Ask Him to free you from all feelings of depression when you feel them coming at you. As the bright beams of His love and righteousness flood into your mind, your depression should continue to evaporate.

10. **Ask Jesus to fight for you when you're too weak to fight**. He has promised to fight for you. *"The Lord will fight for you, and you have only to be still"* (Exodus 14:14). Claim this promise in His name. You'll enjoy the result.

11. **Practice rejoicing in God's promises**. Don't ever forget, *"All things work together for good to them that love the Lord and are called according to his purpose"* (Romans 8:28) The apostle Paul puts it this way, *"Rejoice in the Lord always. I will say it again:*

*Rejoice!"* (Philippians 4:4). Do this even when you don't feel like it. I'm confident you'll enjoy the result.

And now I'd like to share with you what I like to call a *"Depression Buster."* You can experiment with this principle right now if you will.

It's a proven psychological principle that our thoughts impact our actions, even when we're being silly. So I'd like to ask you to act out for just a moment and watch what happens to your mood. **Say these words**: *"I choose to be a happy person today!"* Now say them again with greater enthusiasm. And again—a third time—with a big smile.

Now (assuming you're not in a public library or some meeting), say these words again with super enthusiasm, pumping your fist in the air or raising both hands high as you do so. Blast out these words: *"I CHOOSE TO BE A HAPPY PERSON TODAY!" By the way, whenever you say the words, "I choose..." you're exercising your will. This releases energy into your entire being, enabling these words to become your reality.*

If you weren't feeling very "up" a few minutes ago, did you notice your mood improving (assuming you just did this exercise)? So does this mean that all you have to do is mouth happy words and jump up in the air and you will become more joyful?

To a certain extent, yes. Endorphins are released every time you utter a positive thought or act out in a positive way. But depression is a tough customer, and you'll need more than this exercise to sustain those good feelings over the long haul. So enjoy your brief endorphin release, but let's get back to this cognitive-therapy business.

In his book, *Feeling Good,* Dr. David Burns says that cognitive therapy is a fast-acting technology of mood modification that patients can apply on their own. He says that many who have milder forms of depression can get relief from symptoms in as little as twelve weeks. I find this personally exciting, because I have experienced relief from symptoms of depression myself through a spiritual version of cognitive therapy. Here's an example.

## A Personal Experience

A few years ago, I awakened during the early hours of a Friday morning thoroughly depressed. The heaviness was all over me. I couldn't think; I could barely function. And if I hadn't had to use the bathroom, I might not have gotten out of bed at all. It was still dark, probably around four in the morning. Here's how the experience unfolded.

1. I staggered out to the ottoman in our family room and began to pray. I invited God into my life—something I do every day before doing anything else. Mind you, I was still depressed and on my knees, my face buried in the ottoman.

2. A few moments later, I turned on a very small lamp on the dining room table and opened my Bible. I paged here and there somewhat aimlessly and ended up drifting through some psalms. Psalm 34:18 really caught my attention. *"The Lord is close to the brokenhearted and saves those who are crushed in spirit."* Then I read verse 19: *"A righteous man may have many troubles, but the Lord delivers him from them all."* After reading these promises, I said to the Lord, *"I'd like to claim these for myself."*

3. At this point you may be saying, *"That's nice for him. He's probably a righteous person, but that's not me."* Hey, I'm not righteous either, apart from Jesus. But the Bible tells me that those who commit their lives to Jesus Christ receive Jesus' righteousness as a gift apart from their behavior.

   So I said to God, *"I'm claiming these promises this morning in Jesus' name."* I could do that because Jesus tells us in John 14:13, *"Whatever you ask in my name, I'll do it."* So I told God, *"I'm claiming Jesus' righteousness and these promises for myself."*

4. Now I really was beginning to feel better. I was still half zombie, but I could feel changes taking place inside me. I could sense new life stirring. The next thing I knew, the words of Jeremiah 29:11 popped into my mind: *"'I know the plans that I have for you,' declares the Lord, 'plans to prosper you and not to cause you harm, plans to give you hope and a future.'"* I recited and claimed that promise and thanked God that He would deliver me from all my troubles and for the fact that He still had a plan for my life—a plan to prosper me. Know what happened next? My depression began to dissipate.

Why was I depressed in the first place, you might ask, and why did I find these particular promises so encouraging? Well, I had been out of work for more than two years, and sometimes under such circumstances a person can feel pretty inadequate. Inadequacy is a common way for depressed people to feel. But God had just reminded me that He still had a plan for my life and that He would deliver me from all my troubles.

*And I bought it! Score one for spiritual cognitive therapy, otherwise known as thinking straight. You can do this, too, by exercising your faith in God's promises no matter what your circumstances and feelings may tell you.*

God's promises have tremendous power. If you will practice appropriating them—internalizing them, in other words—they will do wonders in helping you beat back feelings of depression and live a happier, more joyful life.

## An Important Thought

The Bible declares that the Word of God is full of living power (Hebrews 4:12). But like the power contained within a bullet, the power in God's Word is useless unless it is released. You can hold a bullet in your hand all day and nothing will happen. But if you put it in a gun and pull the trigger, all the explosive power in that bullet is unleashed as the firing pin strikes the bullet.

*It is the same with the power in God's Word. The promises of the Bible are full of living power, but that power stays dormant until it is released in your life by the firing pin of the Holy Spirit as you exercise your faith.*

Use the living power in God's Word to shoot down the darkness of depression in your life. Here's how. Jesus said that people need more than physical food in order to live. They must feed on God's Word— every word that comes from God's mouth (Matthew 4:4). *You can feed on God's promises by reading them, memorizing them, and asking the Spirit of God to install them in your life.*

Here specifically is how you can pull the trigger that unleashes the power of His promises. Jesus explains the process like this: *"Whatever you ask for in prayer, believe that you have received it, and it will be yours"* (Mark 11:24). Some have called this the ABCs of prayer. **Ask** God to do what He says He will do, **Believe** that He will, then **Claim** the promise. It is yours by faith.

Remember, it is the exercising of your faith—trusting God to do what He says He will do—that enables the Holy Spirit to unleash God's awesome power in your life against what might otherwise be paralyzing depression. *"Not by might nor by power, but by my Spirit,' says the LORD Almighty"* (Zechariah 4:6).

Here's another personal example. Five mornings a week I try to get up around four, and at 5:20 I head for a workout at a nearby fitness center. It's always a battle. I'm in my 70s, and my body is not particularly interested in two- and three-mile walk-runs anymore. I have arthritis in my knees and probably in my back and hips. Sometimes I hurt all over.

But I have a secret weapon. A magic bullet, if you will. It is found in Isaiah 40:29-31, and I have memorized it so I can feed on it. Here's how it reads: *"He gives power to the faint, and to him who has no might He increases strength. . . . Those who wait on the LORD shall renew their strength; they shall mount up with wings like eagles, they shall run and not be weary, they shall walk and not faint."*

Every morning I claim this promise as I hobble out the door and head for the fitness center. I ask God to make His miracles and mercies fresh and new during my ten-minute drive to the gym. Do I get an immediate rush after ingesting this promise? I don't. But after about five minutes on the treadmill, the miracle begins to happen. My aches and pains begin to fade, and I run and walk the remainder of my two and a half miles with minimal discomfort.

Afterward, I'm loose and feeling better mentally as well. Why? Because thanks to the Word of God, I've had an endorphin release. Physical exertion to the point of sweating releases endorphins into the brain, but so do singing, meditation, and claiming Bible promises. These endorphins elevate our mood and cause us to feel better.

Dr. Glenn Bell, a clinical psychologist friend, tells me that *drop for drop, endorphins are twenty-five times more powerful than morphine.* So after my workout, I can say, *"Hey, I just released 138,000 endorphins!"* It almost makes you want to exercise, no matter how old you are, doesn't it?

I also want to insert the thought that you may be depressed because you need to make a difficult decision about something in your life—

something that drags you down and will continue to do so until you make a decision to change it. Here's a case in point from a friend of my family, in her own words, about a depressing marriage issue.

## Jennifer's Story

"I got married at 18. I was young, very naïve, and came from a loving family with a protective and nurturing father who loved me unconditionally. Silly me, I thought all men were like my father.

"After ten years of marriage, I had some major concerns about my husband's lack of honesty. So I approached him and suggested that he consider getting professional help. I told him that I would stay in the marriage if he would seek counseling. My husband was very controlling and dishonest, and he convinced me that if there was anything wrong with our marriage, it was my fault. He also said that if anyone was crazy, it was me. So he didn't go for counseling. But I did.

"I made an appointment with a psychiatrist who gave me a prescription for antidepressants. They made me worse, so I quit taking them. But I still met with the psychiatrist weekly and talked and cried while he sat and listened. Every once in awhile, I would say, *'My husband told me such and such,'* and the psychiatrist would reply dubiously, *'Oh, really?'* Or *'I doubt that.'*

"To me that meant, *'He doesn't believe my husband either. Maybe I'm not crazy!'* After two months of me talking and crying and the psychiatrist mostly listening, I went into his office one day and said, *'I know what's wrong. It's my husband, and if I don't get away from him, I really will go crazy.'*

*"'I was wondering when you would figure that out,'* he replied.

"I went home and told my husband I wanted a divorce. He responded by breaking my nose."

Now, I don't want to suggest that divorce is the answer to one's marriage problems. (And obviously if you're not married, getting a divorce isn't an option anyway.) My point is that this young woman had something seriously wrong in her life and had to make a difficult decision in order to keep her mental and physical health. Once she made that decision, she told me, her depression evaporated!

If you suffer from symptoms associated with depression, ask yourself if there is an issue in your life that you have been avoiding and need to confront. Perhaps you'll need to make a hard decision before things get better. Additionally, if an area of your life is out of harmony with God's principles, your depression likely won't go away until you fix it.

I stated earlier that God's Word is full of living power and that our faith in His promises releases that power. I believe that with all my heart. But I also realize that it's a lot easier for me to tell you to believe God's promises than it may be for you to do so.

But it's true!

A few years ago, I had been without an income for two and a half years, after selling my company to a national competitor. That was a challenging period for me, and in time depression came calling—frequently. I prayed for God's leading. I applied for jobs in various venues, with no success.

One organization told me (in writing, no less) that I was too old (I was in my 60s). But I kept claiming the beautiful promise in Jeremiah that God still had a plan for my life. I claimed that promise for more than two years—as well as the promise in Psalm 37:4—*"Delight yourself in the LORD and he will give you the desires of your heart."* However, for more than two years, I experienced turndowns by one prospective employer after another. All the while, my mother-in-law was telling Diane, *"Mike needs a job."* Like I didn't know that!

So what do you do when you pray, claim God's promises—and nothing happens? Think about that. Because at some point you will have to go through your own personal Job experience when your faith will be tested, and God won't appear to be around. What are you going to do then?

The correct answer is simple but difficult to implement: *Keep on trusting that all things really do work together for good for those who love the Lord—because that's what the promise says, and God is always true to His promises* (see Romans 8:28).

What happened to me ultimately? you may ask. Well, no one hired me. So my wife, Diane, ended up retaining my services as a house-husband (while she works two days a week). This helps this former businessman stay humble. Most weeks, I do food preparation, dishes, laundry, ironing, clean toilets, and do grocery shopping. I also write books and do some speaking.[2]

How is this paying the bills? Good question. And the answer is with the combination of Diane's and my Social Security checks, coupled with a very modest retirement from a previous employer and occasional speaking fees. We're within a few months of having our home paid for, and (as I'm writing this) we're about to spend two weeks in Paris and London.

As I stated a few sentences back, things really do work together for good for those who love the Lord and try to fit into His plan. We've not become world travelers, by any means. Our primary purpose is to be difference makers in the lives of others. I share how we do this in occasional seminars I present. *That's just one more secret we've discovered on how to beat depression—trying to be there for others, often just by listening and letting them vent and letting them know we care.*

To beat depression, it is terribly important—essential, actually—that we exercise our faith in the face of the most hopeless-looking situations. This not only beats back the forces of darkness that are constantly seeking to enshroud us in depression and discouragement, it also results in a relationship with God. It's the only sensible way to live.

The Bible teaches that you and I will be overcomers only by trusting in God's promises, no matter what our circumstances and feelings are telling us. Believing and acting on this principle is one of the few drug-free ways I know to become free from depression.

## Self-Esteem? What Self-Esteem?

Many who suffer from depression feel inadequate and worthless. So it becomes vital to answer the question: What is the source of our self-esteem? Are we entitled to feel good about ourselves?

Popular psychology often says we need to look for the good within, but as I noted earlier, the Bible tells us that on the inside we are only unwell. *"The whole head is sick"* (Isaiah 1:5). *"The heart is deceitful above all things and desperately wicked"* (Jeremiah 17:9). None of this is likely news to you.

---

2.    But here you are reading my best-selling book.

And it's depressing, isn't it? Except that the Bible also suggests that if God is in our lives, we have a way out and can have a terrific sense of self-esteem. That's because Jesus tells us, *"I have called you friends"* (John 15:15). It's hard to beat that for instilling a sense of self-esteem, don't you think?

The Bible also tells us that He would have each of us be His ambassadors and one of these days sit with Him on His throne and help in the administration of the universe (see Revelation 3:21; 1 Corinthians 6:3; Luke 12:44). As far as we know from Scripture, not even angels get to sit on God's throne! But you and I can have that expectation right out of the Bible!

And now here's what happened to Doug Bloch, whose story of devastating depression I began telling at the beginning of this chapter.

*"I received a phone call from Eddy, the pastoral counselor of a church I was attending."*

Eddy proposed to Doug the idea of a meeting in two weeks that would include himself, Doug, the senior pastor, and members of the prayer ministry of that church. They hoped, Eddy said, that their combined prayers would create a powerful, healing energy for Doug. Doug agreed to meet with them.

*"When I arrived,"* Doug said, *"I described the history of my illness and my feelings of despair. Then the twelve-person group shifted the focus away from my symptoms and asked me to imagine what wellness would look like. Although I could not remember a time when I was not anxious or depressed, I described in as much detail as I could the thoughts, feelings, and behaviors I might experience if I were healed of my affliction.*

*"The group then affirmed that my desire was already a reality and agreed to hold in their consciousness my vision of wellness over the next thirty days until we met again."* He said a total of six monthly support meetings were scheduled.

*"Seventy-two hours after this prayer support began, the black cloud of depression began to lift. Within ninety days, I was completely free of my symptoms."* He concludes, *"If there is a moral to this story, it is that no matter how sophisticated brain science*

*and technology become, there is no substitute for human love and caring...*

"*Every day, I am grateful that a committed group of loving people took a few hours from their busy schedules to give their love and support. Whether I recovered thanks to the power of prayer or simply because of their unfailing encouragement, my struggles with depression are finally over.*"

Today Doug Bloch is a counselor and author of *When Going Through Hell... Don't Stop! A Survivor's Guide to Overcoming Anxiety and Clinical Depression* (Oshweken, Ontario, Canada: Pallas Communications, 1999).

I would like to close this chapter with this Bible promise, which you may remember from the chapter on my near drowning. I consider it a real depression beater:

> "*Fear not, for I have redeemed you, I have called you by name* [your name here], *you are mine; when you pass through the waters, I will be with you, and through the rivers, they will not [drown] you; when you walk through the fire, you will not be burned, neither shall the flame kindle upon you; for I am the Lord Your God, the Holy One of Israel, your Savior...and I love you*" (Isaiah 43:1-4).

You and I may have to battle the darkness of depression for as long as we live in this world. But by letting God change you into a different person every day, you can win these battles. Furthermore, one of these days, the Bible tells you, "*the righteous will shine like the sun in the kingdom of their Father*" (Matthew 13:43), and your depression will be no more.

# CHAPTER FOURTEEN

# How to Forgive a Dirty, Rotten Scumbag!

When I was 17, I left home for the first time and went away to college. I'd never been away for more than a few days at youth camp, and I was apprehensive, insecure, and scared.

I didn't have my first car yet, and my parents drove me to the college I would be attending. When nearly all of my belongings were finally in my dormitory room, I went down to the car for my last two suitcases, and my mother said something I've never forgotten.

*"We don't know why we've brought you here,"* she said. *"We know you're probably going to flunk out."*

*"Thanks a lot, Mother,"* I replied. And half-blinded by tears of fear and outrage, I picked up my last two suitcases and stumbled up the hill to the cockroach-infested old wooden dormitory that was to be my new home. Not only did my childhood come to an end at that moment, but I also acquired a huge forgiveness problem toward my mother that would not be resolved for many years.

Have you ever had a forgiveness issue? A lot of us carry painful wounds that cause us years—sometimes decades—of pain long after they were inflicted. Even if your life experiences have been quite different from mine, you've likely had to deal with at least one or two forgiveness issues along the way—times when someone really hurt you. Or maybe you're the one who did the hurting, and you could use some forgiveness.

Most of us don't get excited when we learn that God instructs us to love our enemies and forgive them. How can we achieve this kind of forgiveness? Why should we—and who wants to, anyway?

The dictionary definition of forgiveness uses expressions such as: *"To give up resentment or claim to requital (payback)." "To pardon one's enemies."* In other words, when I forgive someone, I don't hold onto the wrong he or she has done to me. My attitude toward him or her is the same after the hurt as it was before. We may no longer be palsy-walsy, but I'm not bitter, resentful, or roiling with rage.

Sooner or later all of us need to forgive and be forgiven.

It was Jesus who said, *"Forgive, and you will be forgiven"* (Luke 6:37). He also said that if someone *"sins against you seven times in a day, and seven times comes back to you and says, 'I repent,' forgive him"* (Luke 17:4).

When Peter asked Jesus how often he should forgive someone, Jesus told him seventy times seven, making the point that our forgiveness should be without end (see Matthew 18:21).

Easier said than done, however. Right?

Sooner or later, most of us will experience someone's misconduct that we'll regard as unforgivable. In my case, it took fifteen years before I forgave my mother, not that she ever sought my forgiveness. More about that later. For now, I'd like to focus on the challenges that forgiveness brings to all of us along life's pathway.

Why is it so difficult to forgive?

One reason may be that we want the person who hurt us to know how wrong they were or at least to suffer for what they did. Some who've been hurt in a relationship let the other person know how they feel by seeing how long they can extend the silent treatment. Of course, other methods are available, such as dishing out some pain ourselves, although you wouldn't stoop to doing that, would you?

Let's take a look at God's nature and explore how He forgives. Remember, this is the same nature you and I can have through the "Exchanged Life." Note the forgiveness description in God's portrayal of Himself to Moses: *"The LORD, the LORD, the compassionate and gracious*

*God, slow to anger, abounding in love and faithfulness, maintaining love to thousands, and forgiving wickedness, rebellion, and sin"* (Exodus 34:6).

I would contend that forgiveness is a supernatural gift and that without God in our lives, none of us can forgive the awful stuff that happens to us.

In her wonderful book *Forgiveness: A Bold Choice for a Peaceful Heart*, Robin Casarjian says, *"The most obvious reason for forgiving is to relieve ourselves of the effects of chronic anger and resentment."*

What are the effects of chronic anger and resentment? Hostility, bitterness, and other like feelings grind inside us when we don't forgive. Physical damage begins to occur each time we indulge rage and resentment.

You see, rage, bitterness, and anger are killers. They cause our blood pressure to rise. Chronic high blood pressure erodes our coronary artery walls. Over time, plaque accumulates, which leads to coronary artery disease and finally to premature death. Got an irregular heartbeat? You might do a little introspection to make sure you don't have a bitterness or forgiveness issue.

*On a spiritual level, the arteries of our souls also harden when we don't forgive.* We lose our capacity to love. Those who can't forgive can't love. The unforgiving often have few friends. They're not much fun to be around. Dr. Dean Ornish, in his pioneering book, *Love and Survival*, claims that our literal survival—physically, emotionally, and spiritually—depends on the healing power of love, intimacy, and relationships.

But people who don't—or can't—forgive, are unable to experience genuine intimacy. They can't have healthy relationships. My mother and dad, both now deceased, had forgiveness issues with each other, and their marriage was fifty-five years of war. Mother won most of the battles, but they both lost the war and died younger than they should have.

The Bible talks repeatedly about the importance of forgiveness. Jesus said that if we want God's forgiveness, we must forgive others. *"And when you stand praying, if you hold anything against anyone, forgive him, so that your Father in heaven may forgive you your sins"* (Mark 11:25). So God forgives me to the extent that I forgive? Ouch! What if I can't forgive?

Here's an example based on a true story with names changed.

Bill had a two-year affair with Jim's wife. When it became public knowledge, the affair was the catalyst that led to Jim's marriage breaking up. Over time, Jim became a Christian and remarried. However, years later Bill's name came to Jim's mind one day, and he felt rage welling up. Jim realized he had never forgiven Bill for what he felt was unforgiveable.

Here are the steps that Jim used to forgive Bill. (He had forgiven his ex-wife at an earlier time.)

1. **Jim confessed to God his inability to forgive Bill**. He also admitted that this was wrong, and he sought God's forgiveness for his hatred of Jim over many years.

2. **He asked God to change him into a different person—one capable of forgiving the worst of grievances.**

3. **Jim then asked God to give him His forgiveness for Bill**. He prayed, *"Lord, please change me into a different person. I choose to forgive Bill for his behavior. I also surrender my life to You anew and ask that You will give me Your forgiveness for Bill since I simply don't have it in me to forgive him."*

4. **Jim incorporated the following Scripture into his prayer:** *"Lord, You've said to forgive and I will be forgiven and that if I hold anything against anyone, I must forgive him so that You can forgive me my sins"* (Luke 6:37 and Mark 11:25).

5. **Jim concluded his prayer by saying,** *"Lord, I have done what You said to do. Now I ask that You forgive me for my previous inability to forgive. Please also heal me from any damage my hatred has done to me over the years or to those around me. I ask in Jesus' name."*

Implement this protocol as often as necessary until your being catches up with this faith decision. Even if you don't feel much different at first, the Holy Spirit will bring your decision into an ongoing reality, and you'll experience a new peace and joy in your life.

I emphasize here that you may need to follow the foregoing steps repeatedly in the early going. This is because your new heavenly software may need a certain amount of time to reprogram your ruined hardware (think *brain*) with repeated installations of your decision to forgive.

This is also a wonderful way to experience God in your life. Because, you see, God never gives His gifts apart from Himself.

James Hilton wrote: *"If you forgive people enough, you belong to them and they to you, whether either person likes it or not—squatters rights of the heart."*

Does this mean that I am forced to have a relationship with a person who has damaged me just because I forgive him or her? Not at all. A relationship with such a person is certainly not necessary and might actually be unhelpful.

Here's the rest of my own forgiveness story that involved my mother and me.

You'll remember that she told me as she and dad dropped me off for my freshman year at college that they felt I'd probably flunk out. As I went back to my dorm room after that, I vowed to stay as far away from her as I could until the day she died. I made good on that promise for about fifteen years. I even spent one entire Christmas vacation cleaning bathrooms on the empty university campus, not just to help with my tuition—but also to avoid seeing my mother.

However, about two years after becoming a Christian, I attended a seminar in Philadelphia in which the speaker was talking about the importance of forgiveness. He said it didn't matter who was most to blame in a conflict between two people. Christians had the responsibility, he said, to extend forgiveness. *"Even if the other person was 87 percent wrong,"* he said, *"take care of your 13 percent."*

That got to me.

A few months later I had occasion to visit my parents in Grand Rapids. Not long after I arrived at my parents' house, Mother and I were alone in the living room when I began to do one of the hardest things I have ever done—to ask her forgiveness for my (13 percent) responsibility for the bad blood between us. The conversation went something like this—and includes what I call the six amazing words that can transform relationships.

I told my mother briefly about my commitment to Christ in New York City and that I had something to tell her that came out of that experience.

Then I said, *"Mother, I realize that when I was growing up, I wasn't very nice to you some of the time."*

*"Yes, that's true,"* she replied.

I said, *"I guess I was pretty hard to get along with."*

And she said, *"Yes, that's true, too."*

I continued, *"I must have caused you and Dad quite a bit of pain."*

*"You really did,"* she said, and she got specific about certain incidents I had long forgotten.

Then I told her, *"I'm sorry, Mother. Will you forgive me?"*

And my mother, whom I remember as a feisty little Irish woman who never backed away from a scrap, looked at me in disbelief. Tears filled her eyes, and she forgave me for the boyhood damages I had inflicted.

My relationship with my mother improved considerably after that encounter. It never became great. But I'll tell you this: Something beautiful happens between two people when one person says, *"I'm sorry. Will you forgive me?"* and the other says, *"I forgive you."*

Years of bitterness, resentment, and rancor melted away after Mother and I had that exchange.

You may be wondering if my mother ever made amends for her misconduct. She never did. But, you know, that was *her* problem. It was nice for me to have a decent adult relationship with her after that and not to have to carry around all of the anger and vitriol from my youth. By God's grace and through the Exchanged Life, I forgave her anyway. And keep in mind that I forgave her not because I wanted to but because I needed to.

So are you thinking of someone who has hurt you along the way? Maybe you need to talk to him or her about your 13 percent. If you have such a conviction, pray about it. I've had one situation where I felt it was better simply to forgive a person who had wronged me without actually making contact. In another situation where I had caused pain, I wrote a letter and expressed my deep regret for the pain I had caused, and he forgave me. My entire life was enhanced.

And of course you'll remember the six magic words that can transform relationships? *"I'm sorry. Will you forgive me?"*

A word of caution. If you decide to forgive someone who has hurt you and you say these six magic words, stop there. Don't add, *"You know, none of this would have happened if you hadn't done or said such and such."* Just take care of your part and leave the results with God.

## Marietta Jaeger's Story

I'd like to conclude this chapter with one of the greatest forgiveness stories I have ever read.

Her name was Marietta Jaeger. She and her husband, Bill, and their five children took their first-ever camping vacation in June 1973. They left their home in Detroit and headed west to the Badlands National Park, Mount Rushmore, and the Black Hills of South Dakota. At every rest stop, 7-year-old Susie, their gangly, dark-haired youngest child, practiced cartwheels. Then it was everybody back in the van. Marietta would make a quick head count, and they were off again.

On June 23, they reached Missouri Headwaters State Monument near Three Forks, Montana, and set up camp beside a river rumbling with snow melt.

On the third night Susie and 13-year-old Heidi awoke about two o'clock and whispered awhile before dropping back to sleep. A few hours later, Marietta was roused by a cold breeze on her shoulders. Groggily, she groped to locate the source, and her hand brushed grass where there should have been canvas. A hole had been sliced in the side of the tent. Two of the sleeping bags beside her were still occupied, but Susie was gone. Quickly the alarm spread. The campground lit up.

The next few heart-stopping hours blurred into days and then weeks as the sheriff was notified and then the FBI. Military crews with tracking dogs combed haystacks and outbuildings; search planes droned overhead; boats with nets scoured the nearby river.

Two weeks into the ordeal, the family was still at the camp waiting. It was a search boat with a net that finally undid Marietta Jaeger. Every time the craft stopped, the men on board would reel in the net. At every stop, the young mother feared her daughter's body would be in the haul.

Panic and anger rose in Marietta; her stomach roiled, and a heavy weight seemed to press against her chest. She fought her feelings, but everything she'd been holding in boiled into a murderous rage. When she crawled into her sleeping bag that night, she told her husband that even if the kidnapper returned Susie unharmed, she would gladly kill him with her bare hands.

She lay awake all night.

Then near dawn Marietta heard a voice that told her, *"I don't want you to feel this way."* The message got to her. As a child, she had been taught to love her enemies and pray for those who hurt her. As she pondered the message, the weight on her chest seemed to lift, and her stomach relaxed. She fell into the first deep sleep she had had since Susie vanished. In the morning, nothing had changed. She still wanted to kill the monster who'd snatched her little girl. But she'd opened the door just a crack to the possibility that revenge wasn't the best course.

*Some say this is how forgiveness starts—not with a rush but with a weary willingness to try.*

Five weeks after Susie's abduction, the Jaegers went home, with Marietta counting four heads now instead of five. Back home in Detroit, Bill began packing a gun and sank into silent brooding. For her part, Marietta recalled the flicker of revelation she'd had by the river. And she'd remembered relatives who had died embittered over ancient affronts.

The conclusion was obvious. Hatred of the magnitude she was feeling got people nowhere. So Marietta made the decision to try to forgive. She reminded herself that the kidnapper was as precious in God's eyes as was Susie. That thought was awfully hard to swallow, and her exercise of that thought was largely mechanical.

In another strategy, Marietta found a new way to apply the precept to pray for your enemies. She knew the kidnapper probably lived in the West, and she began wishing him clear skies. Her work became harder each time a development in the case rekindled her rage, such as the day a man called claiming to have Susie, seeking a ransom, then hanging up before he could be identified.

But Marietta persisted in visualizing positive events in the life of the kidnapper—blue skies, or seeing him catch record-sized trout. If the kidnapper had Susie, she wanted him to be content. If he did not, she wanted him to come forth and confess.

The relief she felt when she focused on compassion for the man who had wronged her was more than imaginary. Dr. Joan Borysenko, a biologist from Harvard and a pioneer in studying how emotions affect the body, goes so far as to say that forgiveness is the mind's most powerful healing tool.

How so? Plentiful research now exists showing that hostility is a major risk factor for coronary artery disease and a host of other illnesses. The weight Marietta had originally felt in her chest reflects what was presumably happening in her body as her fury grew. Adrenaline sped into her bloodstream, raising her pulse and her blood pressure. Her arteries narrowed, and the blood surged through her heart. Over time, such stress could be lethal. But that weight had lifted as soon as Marietta made the decision to forgive Susie's kidnapper.

One year almost to the minute that Susie was snatched, the Jaegers phone rang in the middle of the night. Marietta sprinted toward the kitchen in the dark, switched on the tape recorder attached to the phone by the FBI, then grabbed the receiver.

*"Is this Susie's mom?"* the guy asked. *"I'm the guy that took her from you."* The man said he'd read a newspaper article in which Marietta said she wished she could talk to the kidnapper. She could tell by the tone of his voice that he was calling to taunt her. But the man hadn't counted on the forgiveness homework she had been doing every day after lunch.

When she heard the man's voice, she realized that something had genuinely shifted inside her. This man had done something vile, and her child was in dire trouble. Yet the man was also someone's beloved child and in terrible trouble also. The compassion Marietta now felt for him came through in her voice.

She asked evenly if Susie was alive and if he had hurt her. The caller assured her that Susie was fine and added that he had hurt her only a little when he had to choke her to keep her from crying out. As he talked, Marietta could hear the clicks of the FBI tracer on the line, and she knew the caller must be hearing them too. But every time he grew anxious, she gently drew him in again.

*"Can we have her back?"* she asked.

*"I'm in kind of an awkward position to do that,"* he said. *"I've gotten used to her."*

*"Why did you take her?"*

He stammered for a moment, then said, *"I've always wanted a little girl of my own."* But what really brought down the caller's defenses was when Marietta asked with total sincerity, *"What can we do to help you?"*

There was a brief silence. Then she realized the kidnapper was crying.

*"I wish I knew how to answer that,"* he said finally.

Miraculously, the call lasted for more than an hour. But the tracer malfunctioned and located the caller as being in Florida, a dead end. Then the FBI matched a voiceprint of the anniversary call with another call to a suspect in a murder case in the same region where Susie was taken. This suspect was David Meirhofer, a popular babysitter from the small town of Manhattan, Montana.

When Meirhofer was arrested, he confessed to killing Susie about a week after abducting her. He also admitted to having murdered a teenage girl and two young boys. Hours after his confession, he committed suicide.

In the years that followed, Bill Jaeger continued to seethe. He developed bleeding ulcers and heart problems. In 1987 he collapsed on the kitchen floor, dead of a heart attack. He was only 56 years old.

Today, Marietta, a grandmother of seven, radiates good will as she travels around the country giving workshops on forgiveness. In recent years, she has befriended Meirhofer's 71-year-old mother. They even went together to visit their children's graves.

Afterward the two moms sat in the living room sipping coffee and thumbing through old scrapbooks. There was David Meirhofer in one—a rosy-cheeked little boy, scrubbed and eager to set out for his first day of school. And there were Mother's Day cards from a boy his mother remembered only as a doting son.

As she studied the smiling boy in the snapshot, Marietta felt that her struggle to invest the faceless killer of her daughter with humanity was complete. *"If you remain vindictive, you give the offender another victim,"* she says. *"Anger, hatred, and resentment would have taken my life just as surely as Susie's life was taken."*[1]

---

1.    From the journal *Hippocrates,* May, 1998.

If you have a forgiveness issue in your life, I hope you'll fix it. Whether you need to seek forgiveness or extend it, by God's grace do what you need to do. Then you'll receive the kind of healing that will bring you transformation and new life. Jesus referred to this as life in all its fullness. And you and I, empty souls that we are without it, need it desperately!

# CHAPTER FIFTEEN

# Why I Don't Own a Gun

I haven't owned a gun since I was a teenager and had an old .22-caliber rifle. Other than shooting a few pesky sparrows who were competing for the bluebird nests Dad had erected in the field behind our house in Grand Rapids, Michigan, I recall grabbing my gun only one time to protect my family.

The incident happened when I was around 14. One afternoon after work, my father drove into our driveway laying on his car horn. When I went outside to learn why all the horn blowing, he called out to me to get my rifle. Dad had correctly perceived that someone was following him. Turned out this individual thought Dad was trysting with his wife, which was not true. Dad was a pretty faithful kind of guy.

Mother assured the man in no uncertain terms that he was incorrect, and, of course, Dad did the same. When I showed up with my rifle and pointed it toward this individual, the man asked me to put the gun down. Of course, I didn't. Then after few minutes of discussion, he agreed he had made a mistake, apologized, and drove away.

I don't know what ever happened to that old .22. When I left home for college about three years later, I left the gun behind and haven't had one since. Candidly, I haven't felt the need for one during the sixty or so years that have elapsed since that incident.

You see, as a Bible Christian, I believe I have divine protection. I believe you'll see in the several Scriptures which follow why I hold to that viewpoint, especially since I have a biblical worldview. I ingest the promises which follow most every day.

*"No weapon that is formed against you will prosper"* (Isaiah 54:17).

*"Behold I give you power...over all the power of the enemy"* (Luke 10:19).

*"I am your shield and your exceeding great reward"* (Genesis 15:1).

*"The Lord will fight for you, and you have only to be still"* (Exodus 14:14).

*"The angel of the Lord encamps round about them that fear Him, and delivers them"* (Psalm 34:7).

*"The Lord says, 'I will rescue those who love Me, I will protect those who trust in My name. When they call upon Me, I will answer. I will be with them in trouble. I will rescue them and honor them. I will satisfy them with a long life and give them My salvation'"* (Psalm 91:14-16).

These are just a few of many Bible promises offering God's protection to those who trust Him.

Now I understand that even in the Christian community, I am in a minority. I read that a majority of Christians want their guns, and who am I to take away their Second Amendment rights? But I contend that it's likely Christians want guns because 95 percent of them do not have a biblical worldview.[1] I mean, if you thought you had divine protection, why would you need a gun?

I think it's worth noting that the ancient Israelites of the Old Testament always had divine protection against their enemies, as long as they kept faith with God and obeyed His commandments. Why should it be any different today? (P.S.: I do understand they had weapons when they went into battle. But when I reflect on what God did to the Egyptians and their other enemies, I'm pretty clear they didn't need them.)

When my wife and I built our new house eleven years ago in Gresham, Oregon, we had it anointed by a minister acquaintance that it would

---

1.    This is according to George Barna, long-time demographer of Christian behavior and views.

always be a place where those who visited would experience peace and healing. We also asked God to put His hedge of protection about our home.

And while no one has pulled a gun on us along the way, I did seek God's protection and intervention a few years back during a lawsuit when our telephone company was unable to resolve a phone problem at a critical time as I was expanding my business into two major new markets. We won a modest settlement, despite being outgunned by the phone company's prestigious law firm in Seattle.

We were David against Goliath. But after the dust had settled, an amazing event took place. The opposing law firm, which had occupied one of the highest floors of a Seattle skyscraper, collapsed, leaving the managing partner a solo practitioner. I still remember how shocked my small, two-person attorney team was when they told me this had occurred.

Another reason why I feel no need to protect myself and my family with a gun is stories like this one, found in 2 Kings 18 and 19, when the massive army of King Sennacherib of Assyria threatened to overwhelm the Jews of Judah and Jerusalem who had been faithful to God.

Here's how the story ended. When everyone awoke on the day of battle, 185,000 Assyrian soldiers didn't wake up. They were dead, killed by the angel of the Lord during the night.[2] Sennacherib survived and limped home, only to have two of his own sons murder him shortly after he got there.

By the way, I think it's worth noting that the Bible suggests those loyal to God aren't really fighting against flesh and blood when there's trouble. Rather, the Bible says, they fight *against those mighty powers of darkness who rule this world*" (Ephesians 6:12). The Bible adds, *"Use every piece of God's armor to resist the enemy in the time of evil so that after the battle you will be still standing"* (verse 13).

What does the armor of God consist of? The Bible says *"the weapons we fight with are not the weapons of the world"* (2 Corinthians 10:3, 4). Then it lists the following six pieces: (1) the helmet of salvation, (2) the

---

2. *"That night the angel of the Lord went out and put to death 185,000 men in the Assyrian camp"* (2 Kings 19:35).

breastplate of God's righteousness (think armored vest), (3) the belt of truth, (4) the gospel of peace, (5) the shield of faith, and (6) the sword of the Spirit (the Word of God) in your mouth and not your hand (see Ephesians 6).

*The sword of the Spirit in the mouth?* Absolutely! When Jesus returns the second time, the book of Revelation describes Him riding on a white horse with the armies of heaven, and *"out of His mouth comes a sharp sword with which to strike down the nations"* (Revelation 19:15).

Isn't it interesting that the same Jesus who spoke the world into existence[3] will one day use the sword of the Spirit (His Word) to speak the world's nations out of existence before He re-creates the world anew?

Whether you agree with my position about guns or not, hopefully Bible prophecies like this one will help you understand why I personally feel no need to arm myself with a gun against potential adversaries. With God's armor on, can you see why I feel that I have a lot of protection?

Finally, since I claim to be a Bible Christian, perhaps it is fitting that I conclude this chapter with the words of the great apostle Paul, who put it this way: *"Be strong in the Lord and in His mighty power." "Don't be overcome by evil, but overcome evil with good" "No weapon formed against you will prosper"* (Ephesians 6:10; Romans 12:21; Isaiah 54:17). (Actually God, not Paul, made the last promise.)

If you don't pack a gun, it sure is a nice equalizer, isn't it!

---

3.   *"Through Him all things were made"* (John 1:3).

# CHAPTER SIXTEEN

# Silencing Evil Voices

## {A mental healing story}

When I was a young pastor in Portland, Oregon, I once called on a parishioner who heard voices. Some of these voices were next-door neighbors, she told me, and she could hear them talking about her. Of course, this bothered her greatly because their comments were unkind—and she wasn't sure what to do about it.

I had another parishioner in Portland who also heard voices. But I didn't learn about this until several years later when I had occasion to call on her after I was no longer her pastor. She told me this story and gave me permission to tell it in the hope that it might help someone else. If you hear voices or otherwise suffer from mental unwellness, I hope Ede's story will contribute toward your healing and restoration.

Ede's problems first came to light when she was diagnosed with a mental breakdown and had to be hospitalized. Here's what happened.

Her troubles began when she received a brochure in the mail describing the benefits of expanding the mind and being able to communicate with one's own subconscious. The promotional piece said a person could even heal oneself of illnesses by learning the principles in the book being offered.

The ideas appealed to Ede, and she sent for the book. She didn't have much success with the book's self-hypnosis techniques. But she was intrigued by a section on automatic writing. She was successful the first time she tried to do it.

Initially, she was delighted when a being who identified herself as the deceased mother of her husband, Ed, began to communicate with her through the automatic writing process. At first Ede wrote for only an hour or two. But it wasn't long before she found herself writing for hours on end, with endless messages from Ed's mom and then others, until she was exhausted.[1]

One night when she was extremely tired and in bed, she received a signal that someone wanted to come through. However, she was so tired she could hardly respond. And as she lay in bed, the thought crossed her mind that it would be nice if she could *hear* the communication instead of just *thinking* it and having to write it down.

Just as quickly as the thought entered her mind, the reality began. Her mother-in-law's voice seemed to be speaking right into her mind, telling her she loved her and how happy she was they could communicate more directly. Ede said they discussed many happy things.

A few weeks later, the voice of someone who said he was a deceased cousin began talking with her. This was followed by two other voices, one claiming to be a deceased man who had founded a system of scientific handwriting analysis, and the other, a professed physician.

Ede said these two latter voices began to dominate her life to such an extent that she wasn't able to sleep day or night. In fact, if she lay down to catch a nap, even during the day, the voices would awaken her.

One night a voice said, *"I am God. I have a very special work for you. I will guide you and will speak to you directly."* Stunned, she began to doubt and remembered that the Bible declares that God now speaks to us through His Son.

*"You can't be God,"* she answered. *"Who are you?"*

There was a long pause.

The next time Ede heard the voice, she said, it had become evil, hateful, and malicious. It told her it was going to destroy her. One night later, she collapsed, and Ed rushed her to a nearby hospital.

At this point, Ede had been unable to speak for over a month. She

---

1.  Ede didn't know at this time that the Bible overwhelmingly teaches that the dead sleep and *"know not anything"* (Ecclesiastes 9:5) until Jesus returns to resurrect them.

said she hadn't consulted a physician about this because the spirit "doctor" said he would help her. At the hospital, she communicated with a real physician by writing her responses to his questions on a notepad. Throughout this time the voice was telling her that if she stayed at the hospital she would die that night. And she believed it.

Prior to her hospitalization, the minister from the church she was attending had come to visit, at her request, for counsel. He was intrigued by the automatic writing and asked her to produce some samples, which he kept. Should she stop this practice? she asked. He told her he didn't know why she should.

Now, after nearly two months of sleeplessness and having been bedfast for a month, Ede was hospitalized, having trouble breathing and feeling drained. Her doctor told her she would have to stay for at least one month. She agreed.

While waiting for a room assignment, the voice she was hearing told her to hold her breath, then forced her to do so until she collapsed.

Hospital attendants carried her to her room, where she became temporarily blind. She couldn't respond to their questions. But that night, heavily sedated, she slept for the first time in nearly two months. She awoke the next day to find herself with high blood pressure, a condition that would plague her for the next eleven years.

Ede had her Bible with her, but the voices threatened to destroy her if she read it. She read it anyway.

Her doctors put her on Stelazine, a powerful drug used to control psychosis. She said it seemed to paralyze her mind. She also was given a drug called Thorazine in heavy doses. With the help of these drugs, Ede slept in a drugged state for most of the next eleven years.

But while the voices could no longer get through, she began to be tormented by evil apparitions every night. However, the voices never came back.

Ede's doctors told her that she would be on the two medications for the rest of her life. She must never fail to take them, she was told, or she would break down again.

She didn't doubt her doctors because, despite the medications, she was experiencing at least one visitation every night. The doctors called them hallucinations. Whatever they were, Ede says they were unspeakably evil and very real. She says she always felt their strong presence before she saw them.

Ede and Ed always kept a light on in the bedroom at night so that the room was never really dark. This eliminated for her the theory that her problem was just an excited imagination brought on by darkness.

Then one day after eleven years of medication and torment, Ede began to experience a miracle. She awoke one morning to feel a delightful surge of strength and energy moving through her body. When she stepped on a scale, she found herself losing weight for the first time in years.

Each day thereafter, she felt increasing improvement. Overweight for years, Ede was thrilled to watch the pounds melting away.

But this was just the beginning.

Several weeks later, she suffered the most blood-chilling visitation she had ever experienced. The same dread of night was in her heart, just as it had been for the previous eleven years as Ede prepared for bed.

Then it happened. As she took out her bottle of medications and prepared to take one, a gentle whisper that seemed to come from deep within her said simply, *"You don't need these anymore."*

Ede was stunned. Panic, fear, and uncertainty welled up within her. She knew the consequences of not taking that little pill. And for several minutes she struggled.

Then she put the medication away and went to bed. Before attempting to sleep, however, she prayed a short, simple prayer: *"Lord, I am putting myself in Your hands. I am trusting You to protect me through the night. Thank You for making me well."*

Almost immediately, she fell into a sweet, refreshing sleep. The next day she praised God for what she sensed He was doing for her.

But God wasn't finished yet.

One morning two weeks later, as Ede started to take her daily dose of Stelazine—the drug the doctors had said she must never miss taking— she heard the same soft whisper, *"You don't need these anymore."*

Although the Lord made it very clear to her that she should withdraw from that drug gradually, she felt that her healing was complete. Indeed, after two weeks of reducing her daily dosage to zero, she was free. The voices never came back.

In the letter she wrote to me describing her experience, Ede said, *"God had stepped in after all the many years of torment and said to Satan and his demons, 'Enough.' And I was free. I had no more fear, no more constant struggle for mental and spiritual survival.*

*"I don't understand why God permitted me to go through such a desperate struggle for so many years before He stepped in and rescued me,"* she said. *"But I do know He had a good reason which I will understand someday. Nonetheless, He was with me through the entire experience, and I am so grateful He didn't allow me to be destroyed."*

Ede told me she is willing for her story to be told in the hope that it might also help someone else who may have mental-health issues. *"God really is available for help and healing,"* she said.

Both physicians who treated her told Ede they regard her restoration as a miracle.

The last time I saw Ede, she told me that her blood pressure was now normal. Her triglyceride count, which had been over 3,000, was under 200. She was energetic, happy, and in the words of her husband, Ed, *"a completely changed person."* She also had just started taking college courses in accounting and tax preparation.

Ede agrees with Ed that she really did become a brand-new person, which, of course, is what this book is all about.

~ ~ ~ ~ ~ ~ ~ ~ ~ ~ ~ ~ ~

Note. In the for-what-it's-worth department, several years before I met Ede, I walked the grounds of a psychiatric hospital in Ohio one day with the medical director and was surprised when he told me that most of the patients there could get better and go home fairly quickly if they would. *"They don't choose to get better,"* he told me, *"and so they stay here for a long time."*

I share this sad fact with you while pointing out that if you are mentally ill, you might have a different outcome by choosing to get better. If you're on medications, am I suggesting you drop your meds? I am not! No hasty decisions, please. Just choose to get better, keep listening to your physician, and ask your Creator-God to guide you. Perhaps in His great mercy and love, He will silence any voices of darkness that may be tormenting you and lead you into "His marvelous light" (1 Peter 2:9).

To help you on your journey, start reading the *"Healing-for-Your-Mind Protocol"* which follows. I'll be praying for you.

## A Healing-for-Your-Mind Protocol[1]

1.  **Invite God into your life every morning before you do anything else.** Jesus says in the Bible, *"I stand at the door and knock. If anyone opens the door, I will come in."*—Revelation 3:20. So tell Him, *"Jesus, please come in. I choose to give You unrestricted access into my life and to surrender my will to Your will. I acknowledge that I don't think straight and need a healed mind."*

2.  **Ask God to give you a new heart and to install His mind in place of your mind.** Just say, *"Lord, You've promised to give me a new heart and said that as a Christian I can have the mind of Christ. Please give me these two gifts today through your indwelling Holy Spirit"* (Ezekiel 36:26; 1 Corinthians 2:16) so that I can think correctly.

3.  **Ask Jesus to evict any powers of darkness that might be in your life and light up your life with the Holy Spirit.** *"Not by power nor by might, but by My Spirit, says the Lord."*—Zechariah 4:6.

4.  **Invite Jesus to change you into a different person.** Just tell Him, "Lord, you told Saul in the Old Testament, *'The Spirit of the Lord will come upon you with power...and you will be changed into a different person.'*—1 Samuel 10:6. Please change

---

1.  The protocol here is deliberately similar to that in chapter 9 ("How to Think Straight"), because they both relate to similar subject matter.

me into a different person, too, so that I might become more like You in character and in conduct."

5. **Jeremiah once wrote,** *"When Your words came, I ate them. They were my joy and my heart's delight."*—Jeremiah 15:16. For example, here's how you can "eat" (receive) promises such as the following example: Just say, "Lord, You've said, *'For God did not give* [me] *a spirit of fear, but a spirit of power, and of love, and of a sound mind* (2 Timothy 1:7). I claim this promise of a sound mind in Jesus' wonderful name."

## Here are some additional promises you might practice "eating" (receiving into your being):

▶ **If you're tempted to fight:** *"The Lord will fight for you, and you have only to be still."*—Exodus 14:14.

▶ **When you're unsure what to do:** *"I will teach you and instruct you in the way you should go."*—Psalm 32:8.

▶ **When you're feeling lonely:** *"I will never leave you nor forsake you."*—Hebrews 13:5.

▶ **Why "eating" God's Word is a good idea:** *"The word of God is full of living power."*—Hebrews 4:12.

▶ **When you're feeling empty:** *"God has given us the Holy Spirit to fill our hearts with His love."*—Romans 5:5.

▶ **If you're tempted to use:** *"Don't get drunk.... Instead, be filled with the Spirit."*—Ephesians 5:18.

▶ **When you're anxious or dissatisfied:** *"Don't be afraid. I am your shield and your exceeding great reward."*— Genesis 15:1.

6. **Every morning thank God for one to five things.** For starters, you might thank God for another day of life. Choosing to have an attitude of gratitude will bring healing to your entire being.

7. **Do something nice for someone today.** This can be as simple as saying hi to a stranger and smiling. Doing little deeds of

kindness will light up your life and bring healing to your mind. This is what the Bible means when it says, *"God blesses those who are merciful, for they will be shown mercy"* (**Matthew 5:7**).

Process each of these points for seven straight days and see if you don't begin to experience a healed mind as God floods your life with His light and love.

# CHAPTER SEVENTEEN

# How to Beat Your Panic Attacks and Anxiety Disorder

I was a 29-year-old marketing executive on the climb and living in Worthington, Ohio, the day my heart went crazy. I was in my car going about thirty-five and heading for an appointment, when out of the blue my heart started going ninety miles per hour. When it didn't stop after twenty to thirty seconds, I had a terrible feeling of dread: *"I'm having a heart attack!"*

I headed straight for my physician's office, raced into her waiting room, and told the staff my heart wasn't beating right. Moments later, Dr. Bixel had her stethoscope on my chest. By then my heart had stopped racing. A number of questions later, she suggested that I might have experienced a panic attack, since my heart seemed fine. Later she asked me about stressors in my life and suggested I might want to consider making an appointment with a mental health professional.

I did exactly what she recommended. But I also quit smoking cigarettes, cut back on my coffee drinking, and started jogging three days a week. That was my one and only panic attack. It occurred back in 1968, but I've never forgotten it. And neither have you if you've ever had one of these traumatic events.

By definition, a panic attack is an episode of extremely intense anxiety, punctuated by feelings of dread, fright, or impending doom. Symptoms can include sweating, trembling, chest pain, palpitations, difficulty in breathing, and flushing. One in three persons experiences a panic attack every year. Episodes frequently come out of the blue, peak quickly, and usually last no longer than ten minutes.

Left untreated, panic attacks can lead to panic disorder, which can ruin lives, destroy careers, and shatter marriages and families. However, appropriate treatment enables 90 percent of those afflicted to improve significantly or achieve a full recovery. Happily, cognitive-behavioral therapy has proved to be a most effective tool, often getting patients to successful outcomes without medication.[1]

In recent years, I've had occasional encounters with individuals suffering from panic attacks. One who comes to mind was Amy, a 25-year-old single mother of two. When I first met her, Amy was working in a mailbox business in a Vancouver, Washington, shopping center. I was mailing some packages, and in the course of our conversation, asked her how everything was going in her life.

*"Okay, I guess,"* she replied.

I picked up on the lack of enthusiasm in her voice. *"Sounds like you've had better days,"* I said.

*"Well,"* she admitted, *"I've been having panic attacks."*

*"Tell me about them,"* I said. And since there were no other customers in the store, she did. Amy said her panic attacks had started six or eight months earlier. She had no idea why. But they had gotten progressively worse.

*"Just a few days ago,"* she said, *"a panic attack hit me, and I had to ask a customer to excuse me while I put my head down on the counter. I just couldn't function. It's not only embarrassing,"* she continued, *"but if I can't get over this, I'll probably lose my job."*

I asked Amy if she was seeing a physician for her problem. She said she wasn't. She didn't want to take medications, she said. She just wanted to get better.

I asked her if she had confidence in the Bible. She replied that she'd been raised Catholic but no longer attended church. She said she had a Bible at home.

---

1.  From Roger Granat, M.D., Associate Professor of Psychiatry, Cornell University Medical College, *If You Think You Have Panic Disorder.*

I told her I was willing to put some information together that I thought might help her. If I did that, I asked, would she be willing to read it?

She said she would.

So I began researching about panic attacks and anxiety disorders.[2] Then a few weeks later, I put together some material from the Bible that I thought might help her. I asked a retired lady in my church who had herself suffered from panic attacks if she would join me in presenting this material to Amy.

She agreed, and the two of us took Amy to lunch and shared what you are about to read. A week later I dropped by Amy's workplace, and she reported she was doing much better but still having occasional panic attacks.

In response to what she told me, I prepared another presentation so she could take the offensive against these attacks rather than just waiting for them to happen. I wanted to see if I could teach her how to use Bible promises like bullets to shoot down her panic attacks.

A week after I left the second presentation with her, Amy reported that she hadn't experienced any further episodes. Months later, when I moved from the area and saw her for the last time, I was delighted to hear Amy say she was totally free from panic attacks.

If you or someone you know suffers from panic attacks, please consider these two presentations that I shared with Amy.

## God's Prescription for Panic Attacks

**Treatment.** The following spiritual treatment is based on the theory that how we think determines how we feel. This model works only if the assumption is accepted that God is trustworthy, actively involved in our lives, and that His promises in the Bible are certain. This recommendation does not preclude psychological counseling, use of medication, or a physical examination by your physician to evaluate for possible brain damage or disease.

**God's treatment for panic attacks is based on trust in His promises.** *"The word of God is full of living power,"* the Bible tells us in Hebrews 4:12.

---

2.  David D. Burns, M.D. *When Panic Attacks*. This book contains outstanding information for helping those suffering from panic attacks. I recommend it highly.

In Matthew 4:4, Jesus says that people need more than physical food to sustain life—they must *feed* on every word from God. What follows is a short list of words from God—Bible promises—*that once you ingest/ receive them*, should help eradicate fear and panic.

Internalize these promises by claiming them as your own. They *are* yours if you believe them, are yours if you receive them. Keep in mind that they come straight from the heart of God to you. Start your day with them by asking God to make them a reality in your life through the Holy Spirit before any panic attacks show up.

For instance, begin your day by claiming this promise: *"The LORD is my light and my salvation; whom shall I fear? The LORD is the strength of my life; of whom shall I be afraid?"* (Psalm 27:1).

Then continue your day by placing your life within the protection provided by God's holy name. *"The name of the Lord is a strong tower; the righteous run to it and are safe"* (Proverbs 18:10).

If panic strikes, claim this promise: *"The LORD will fight for you; you need only to be still"* (Exodus 14:14).

**Remember, with Jesus you are never without protection, including that of angels.** *"The angel of the LORD encamps around those who fear him, and he delivers them"* (Psalm 34:7).

**As an antidote to panic and anxiety, Jesus promises a special kind of peace that surpasses understanding.** In John 14:27, He says, *"Peace I leave with you; my peace I give you. I do not give you as the world gives. Don't let your heart be troubled and don't be afraid."* The apostle Paul explains that this is a special peace that will fend off fear and panic. *"And the peace of God, which passes all understanding, will keep your heart and mind in Christ Jesus"* (Philippians 4:7).

**Keeping God in our thoughts is another key for staving off panic attacks, according to Isaiah 26:3.** *"You will keep him in perfect peace, whose mind is stayed on You because he trusts in You"* (Isaiah 26:3). Tell God, *"I choose to trust You. Please give me your perfect peace."*

**Always use the name of Jesus when claiming God's promises.** Jesus tells us, *"You may ask me for anything in my name, and I'll do it"* (John 14:14).

**Read Psalm 91:14-16 at the beginning of each new day and believe what God tells you there.** Here it is.

*"The Lord says, I will rescue those who love Me; I will protect those who trust in My name. When they call upon Me, I will answer. I will be with them in trouble. I will rescue them and honor them. I will satisfy them with a long life and give them my salvation."*

Then before you start your day, read Ephesians 6:12-17 and follow the instructions about putting on the whole armor of God—all six pieces.

Your entitlement to these and other Bible promises comes through Jesus Christ, who died for your sins. If you're not clear on how to have a relationship with Him, it works like this. If you choose to accept Him as your Savior from all sin and as the Lord of your life, He will give you eternal life right now. He will also give you a new heart (a new nature) through His Holy Spirit.

He promises, *"I will give you a new heart and put within you a right spirit"* (Ezekiel 36:26). This decision should be renewed daily. Review chapter 4 often to enrich your commitment.

**Some other helpful ideas:** For anxiety issues, physicians often recommend a Vitamin B supplement, particularly one that is high in niacin. Whole unprocessed grains are rich in niacin. Also, a modest daily exercise program will release endorphins, serotonin, and dopamine into your bloodstream. These are chemicals that create a sense of well-being and regulate the panic-producing areas of the brain. Stay away from caffeine, nicotine, and other stimulants.

Begin your day by placing your life within the fortress that is God's holy name. Never try to face what you know is going to be a stressful day without prayer. Prayer will pay big dividends in minimizing negative feelings, anxiety, and panic.

One final Bible promise: *"For God has not given us a spirit of fear, but of power and of love and of a sound mind"* (2 Timothy 1:7). The next time you're facing a panic attack, recite this promise out loud, claim it as your own, and say, *"In the name of Jesus Christ, I choose to reject all anxious feelings."* Then watch what happens.

## How to fire God's Spiritual Weapons Against Panic Attacks

Here are some spiritual bullets that helped Amy shoot down her panic attacks. Give them a try if you suffer from panic attacks.

▶ **Bullet #1: Begin your day by inviting God into your life, giving Him full control of you and your day.** Tell Him, *"Lord, I choose to give You full control of my life today, and I seek Your protecting presence all day long."*

▶ **Bullet #2: When you feel a panic attack coming on, pause quickly to remember that you have a divine force field around you.** You really do. The Bible promises, *"The name of the Lord is a strong tower; the righteous run to it and are safe"* (Proverbs 18:10). And God tells us, *"I am your shield and your exceeding great reward"* (Genesis 15:1).

▶ **Bullet #3: God's promises are spiritual bullets that can shoot down panic attacks.** But it is the exercise of your faith that pulls the trigger and brings victory in battle. When you sense a panic attack coming at you, claim these promises and say, *"Jesus, I choose to trust You when You say: 'The LORD will fight for you; you have only to be still'"* (Exodus 14:14). Ask Him, *"Lord, please fight for me right now."* Then relax and cool your jets and let God do what He's promised to do.

Here is another promise for you to ingest:

*"And the peace of God, which passes all understanding, will keep your heart and your mind in Christ Jesus"* (Philippians 4:7).

After Jesus has dealt with your panic attack, ask Him to leave one of heaven's angels behind to protect you. Then praise God for shooting down your panic attack and flooding your life with His peace. Satan hates it when people praise God.

As you systematically claim God's promises every day, you should soon see panic attacks become a part of your past. If this doesn't happen within a week or two, schedule an appointment with your physician for a physical checkup.

Here's more good news. As you invite God into your life, He will then have the right to guide you into the exciting plan that He has for your life.

After all, He promises, *"'For I know the plans that I have for you,' declares the Lord, 'plans to prosper you and not to harm you, plans to give you hope and a future'"* (Jeremiah 29:11).

And now for your easy reference, here are some promises straight from the heart of God that helped Amy. Why not review them every day and try to start memorizing your favorites. God wants you to receive and enjoy each promise.

*"Fear not, for I am with you, be not dismayed, for I am your God; I will help you, I will strengthen you, I will uphold you with my victorious right hand"* (Isaiah 41:10).

*"I am your shield and your exceeding great reward"* (Genesis 15:1).

*"The Lord will fight for you, and you have only to be still"* (Exodus 14:14).

*"The angel of the Lord encamps round about those who fear Him, and He delivers them"* (Psalm 34:7).

*"Peace I leave with you; My peace I give you, not as the world gives. Do not let your heart be troubled and do not be afraid"* (John 14:27).

*"The Lord says, I will rescue those who love Me; I will protect those who trust in My name. When they call upon Me, I will answer. I will be with them in trouble. I will rescue them and honor them. I will satisfy them with a long life and give them My salvation"* (Psalm 91:14-16).

# CHAPTER EIGHTEEN

# A Few Thoughts About Jesus' Final Thoughts

Recently I wondered what Jesus' final thoughts may have been during that last hour before He left heaven to come here. In a stunning reversal of what this book espouses, Jesus is about to exchange His divine life for one like ours. He's about to become one of us so He can die and we can live.

Consider the implications. He is God, Creator of the universe, the self-existing One. There is nothing He doesn't know, yet soon He will know nothing. In less than an hour, Jesus will give up His spectacular heavenly body forever. Soon He will be *"God with us"* in an amazing way—a fetus in the tummy of a Jewish peasant girl, likely a teenager.

He knows He won't be a Tom Cruise or a Brad Pitt. But at this moment He makes those guys look pretty blah. He is still the fairest of ten thousand, the most striking being in existence. Here's what Jesus looked like when He appeared to John, His last surviving disciple:

> *"His head and His hair were white like wool, as white as snow. And His eyes were bright like flames of fire. His feet were as bright as bronze refined in a furnace, and His voice thundered like mighty ocean waves.... And His face was as bright as the sun in all its brilliance"* (Revelation 1:14, 16).

Keep in mind that this spectacular Being won't *"consider equality with God something to be grasped, but will make Himself nothing...and become obedient to death—even death on a cross"* (Philippians 2:6-8).

The Bible makes clear that once Jesus gets here, He will be quite plain, having *"no beauty that we should desire Him."*[1] It will be quite a comedown once His heavenly body is gone, and He will never get it back. You see, God didn't just *loan* His Son to the human race, He *gave* Him to us.

For a few more minutes, Jesus is omnipotent. He can still speak worlds and galaxies into existence. *"All things were made by him,"* the Bible says. But saving, not creating, is His focus now. He who made everything is just moments away from setting aside His incomprehensible power for a stunning nine-month blackout.

During the next step in the rescue operation of the ages, He will be unconscious in Mary's womb. It will be an almost incomprehensible state for a Being who at the moment can *"fill the whole universe"*[2] with His presence. Many scholars believe He won't even know who He is for the first twelve years after He gets here.

For the moment, however, He's still omniscient, with the most magnificent mind in the universe. If He chooses, He can launch His awesome intellect forward a hundred million—or a hundred billion—years to consider beings He will one day create. Just now, perhaps He is only gazing thirty-one years ahead as He calls out Peter, James, John, Judas… Why in the world will Jesus reach out to that sociopath Judas? That's the guy who will betray Him.

Perhaps it will be an attempt to reach you and me who may have some of the same tendencies.

Even a year from now He will only have the mind of a cooing, drooling baby needing His diaper changed. A baby born in a barn!

When He is 12 He will understand who He is for the first time and why He's here. But His memories of heaven will remain hidden from Him. In heaven, He's been the center of attention, adored by His Father, worshiped by angels. But soon He will be the focus mainly of His impoverished parents, some shepherds, a few wise men, and of the demons He once created as angels, who will be trying to kill Him throughout His earthly life.

He's the Son of God, but soon He'll become the Son of man. Like us,

---

1.    Isaiah 53:2.
2.    Ephesians 4:10.

He will be subject to headaches, colds, the flu, and worse. Far worse! Far worse, of course, will include His ghastly second death, separated from God the Father while on the Cross so that you and I need never know that horror. That's what hell is really all about—eternal separation from God. Who in his right mind would choose that?

As the countdown continues, He sees His life's closing scenes spiraling downward into the six hours of hell He'll endure nailed to a cross. There He'll hang and bleed until His heart breaks and He plunges into darkness.

Jesus sees it all clearly, but He'll leave anyway. He has to. Because, you see, He is God—and God is love. Which means He won't give us up even if it costs Him His life—and it will. Besides, He's known from eternity this moment was coming. After all, He's the Lamb of God *"slain from the foundation of the world."*[3]

Now the hour is up. Perhaps there's a last embrace with His Father (They've never been apart before) and Jesus disappears from the universe. And neither heaven nor earth will ever be the same again.[4]

Open your life to Him every day as your Savior and Lord, and your life won't be the same again either.

---

3.    Revelation 13:8.

4.    The reason heaven and earth will never be the same again is Jesus' promise to those who commit to Him: *"I'm going to prepare a place for you.... When everything is ready, I will come and get you." "I will invite everyone who is victorious to sit with Me on my throne,"* and *"I am coming soon"* (John 14:2, 3; Revelation 3:21; 22:20).

# Preparing to Meet Jesus

Virtually all of the predictions Jesus made that would precede His return to earth have taken place. He said conditions on earth would be much like they were in Noah's time just before God destroyed the world with a flood. *"Now the earth had become corrupt in God's sight, and it was filled with violence"* (Genesis 6:11).

Jesus said, *"As it was in the days of Noah, so will be the coming of the Son of man."* People were partying the night before and doing their own thing when the Flood came. Everything seemed normal. *"[They] didn't realize what was going to happen until the flood came and swept them all away,"* He said. (See Matthew 24:37.)

You don't have to have an advanced theological degree to know that we're living in a time similar to Noah's, do you?

In this context, I contended earlier in this book that a majority of modern Christian churches fail to teach the complete gospel message of the Bible and other important Bible truths. I'll list just a few here. One huge issue in Christianity is this: Just saying Yes to Jesus doesn't cut it. You also have to die daily to who you are by birth in order to live fully in a saving love relationship with Him.

Jesus wants to replace you with a very different kind of life—life as it is in the Godhead —and He can't do that if you're full of yourself.[1]

---

1.   Chapter 4 is where I attempt to explain how this daily spiritual metamorphosis takes place.

I also suggested that saying you believe in Jesus as your Savior and starting to attend church is the beginning, not the end of being a Christian. I cited demographer George Barna's years of research providing the painful information that most Christians are no different in their conduct from those who make no profession.

My over-arching concern is that a majority of Christian churches do not rely on the Bible exclusively for what they teach. This results in confusion in areas where clarity is vital. Several years ago a British Broadcasting survey in England found that only three of 103 church leaders said they believed in the literal biblical account of a seven-day creation of the world. And only thirteen of the 103 said they believed in a literal Adam and Eve.

I was unable to find specific statistics for America but suspect the results would be similar. This leaves in the lurch, then, the individual who might wish to connect with a denomination offering 100 percent Bible-based doctrines. Some say they do. But you need to check them out because most don't.

Next you will find five important areas where modern churches are frequently unbiblical in the doctrines they espouse. Most churches today, for instance, do not subscribe to what the Bible teaches in these important categories:

1. **What the Bible teaches about creation.**

    a. The Bible teaches that God spoke the world into existence in a literal seven-day week.

    b. Many, if not most, churches teach an unbiblical, much-longer creation process that is in some cases thousands of years long.

2. **What the Bible teaches about death.**

    a. The Bible teaches that death is a cessation of life.

    b. Almost all mainstream churches teach the unbiblical doctrine that the soul is immortal. The Bible is clear this isn't so and states, *"The soul that sins, it shall die"* (Ezekiel 18:4). *"Fear him who can destroy both body and soul in hell"* (Matthew 10:18).

3. **What the Bible teaches about hell.**

a. The Bible says hell is a place of death, i.e., a hole in the ground, a pit, a grave, a garbage dump.

b. Most mainstream churches teach that hell is a place where the lost will burn throughout eternity. The Bible teaches that the wages of sin is death, not eternal burning.[2]

4. **What the Bible teaches about God's commandments.**

a. Jesus says, *"Don't think I have come to abolish the law.... I tell you the truth, until heaven and earth pass away, not the smallest letter, not the least stroke of a pen, will be any means pass away from the law until everything is accomplished." "If you love Me, keep My Commandments"* (Matthew 5:17, 18; John 14:15).

b. Most churches teach we're no longer under the law, that the Old Covenant (the Ten Commandments) has been done away with. The Bible identifies those who avoid the Mark of the Beast at the end of time as the ones who love Jesus so much they *"obey God's commandments and remain faithful to Jesus"* (Revelation 14:12).

5. **What the Bible teaches about Jesus' Second Coming.**

a. The Bible teaches that Jesus will return **once** to resurrect the righteous dead and translate the righteous living and take them to heaven.

b. Many churches today hold the doctrine that Jesus will return **twice,** once in secret and then seven years later to give those who weren't prepared the first time a second chance. That is simply unbiblical.

I'd like to share the following anecdote with you as an illustration of how important it is to be biblical in your belief system and the danger of simply following the teachings of a pastor or church. On a recent trip to Paris, Diane and I were told to take Bus #69 to reach a particular destination. We were also told to take Bus #69 to return to our hotel. It all seemed obvious, and we proceeded accordingly.

---

2. I am familiar with the texts about eternal fire and happy to answer your questions about them.

After reaching our destination and seeing the sites there, we caught another Bus #69 to come back. However, after proceeding on this bus in what turned out to be a totally wrong direction (though we didn't recognize that at first), we found ourselves terribly lost with darkness falling.

Mercifully, another rider told us we needed to get off the bus—that we were at the end of the line. Mystified, we did and started asking the locals—mostly French-speaking folks—for help on how to return to our hotel.

What had gone wrong? Turns out there were *two* Bus #69s! And each went in opposite directions.

No one had explained this to us when we started out. Until someone did, we stayed terribly lost even though we thought we were doing the right thing. Everything changed once we learned the truth of the matter.

In our walk with God, we need to know the truth of the matter. Just as Lucifer did in heaven, *WE* make the call on what *We* think is right or wrong. But sometimes what appears to be right can end up be terribly wrong. This won't happen if we stay biblical. We'll be in the right place when we let the Bible guide us in all our beliefs.

As our planet deteriorates and storms and shootings abound more and more, I predict that one of these days soon there will be a call that we need God in our lives and we need to start attending church again. In other words, a spiritual awakening will occur.

Be glad and be careful when that happens. For historically that which is genuine almost always is superseded by a counterfeit. How can you know the difference and hook up with the genuine?

Let the Bible be your guide in your search for truth as if your life depended on it. It does.

For instance, if you're looking for a church home and you've begun exchanging your old life for a new one every day, look for a church that is true to the Word of God for all of its major doctrines. Until then, study for yourself what the Bible teaches about the important doctrines of the Bible[3] and incorporate them into your life.

---

3.  I can be reached at mjones@paclink.com or at mjonespdx1@gmail.com.

This need not be overly complicated. The last book of the Bible says that those living at the end of time will have the faith of Jesus and will be obeying all of His commandments[4] when He returns. Here are His final words in the last book of the Bible:

*"I am coming soon"* (Revelation 22:20).

---

4. *"Here is the patience of the saints: here are they that keep the commandments of God and the faith of Jesus"* (Revelation 14:12). Seventh-day Adventists are the most biblical group I have found so far.

# Praying Yourself to Death

## (A metamorphosis into a new life[1])

**M**el woke with a start. Groggily, he peered at his alarm clock. Four o'clock in the morning. Groan! His mind still befogged, Mel slipped out of his warm bed and headed for the ottoman in the living room—his place of prayer every morning.

*"Good morning, Lord,"* he began. *"It's your son, Mel, down here in the war zone of Planet Earth, coming in the name of Jesus Christ before Your throne of grace to thank You for another day of life and to invite You to take Your rightful position on the throne of my life.*

"I can barely function, Lord. So please send the Holy Spirit into my life to refresh and revive me and to give me new life this morning, the kind of life Jesus promised—life in all its fullness.

"Father, Scripture tells me you 'give power to the faint and to him who has no might, You increase strength. Those who wait for the Lord,' You've said, 'shall renew their strength. They shall mount up with wings like eagles; they shall run and not be weary, they shall walk and not faint' (Isaiah 40:29-31). May these words become my reality this morning, I pray.

---

1.   Yes, praying yourself to death—but actually metamorphosing into a new life in Jesus. This is how I pray an "Exchanged Life" prayer. I offer it as one example for those who haven't prayed this way before.

*"You have also said, 'I stand at the door and knock. If anyone hears my voice and opens the door, I will come in and eat with him, and he with me'* (Revelation 3:20). *'Please come in, Lord, and guide me into the master plan that You have in mind for me today. I choose to give You unrestricted access into my life and lay all my plans for this day at Your feet.*

*"Please anoint my life with Your amazing grace. You have said, 'My grace is sufficient for you, for my power is made perfect in weakness'* (2 Corinthians 12:9). *'I've got the weakness, Lord, and You've got the power. So please help me to live a balanced life today so that Your power can be made perfect in my weakness.*

"Father, I acknowledge my snakebit condition apart from You. I'm also reminded that the ancient Israelites, when they were literally snake-bitten because of their rebellion, were told to look at a bronze snake hanging on a pole. I know that the snake was a symbol of their sin but also of a Savior who would become sin for them. And as they exercised their faith in Your instruction and looked at the snake, they were healed.

*"Father, my condition is no better than theirs, for apart from You, I am rebellious and selfish. So I come now to the foot of the Cross of Your Son Jesus Christ to follow the instruction of the Bible to behold 'the Lamb of God slain from the creation of the world'* (Revelation 13:8) *and to remember that He 'Himself bore my sins in His body on the tree, so that I might die to sins and live to righteousness'* (1 Peter 2:24).

*"Father, I choose to die to sin and live to righteousness. Please send the Holy Spirit to make my choice a reality as You mediate for me the merits of the Savior's sacrifice and shed blood. Thank You that because of His wounds, I have now been healed. Please heal me in body, mind, and spirit.*

*"Lord, You have said that for my sake You 'made him who had no sin to be sin, so that* **in him** *I might become the righteousness of God'* (2 Corinthians 5:21). *May these words become my reality right now as I accept Jesus anew as my Savior and Lord. And please guide my thoughts as I pause to remember that the experience of Abraham, who was told to sacrifice his son, Isaac, actually became a reality for You at the Cross as You destroyed my sins in the person of Your dear Son Jesus and redeemed me.*

*"My Lord and Savior, I love You and just want to praise and bless Your wonderful name. I pray now that the words of the apostle Paul will become my reality, when he said: 'I've been crucified with Christ; it's no longer I who live, but Christ who lives in me. And the life I now live in the flesh, I live by faith in the Son of God, who loved me and gave himself for me'* (Galatians 2:20).

*"Dear Holy Spirit, please make these words my reality today. Give me a new heart just as You promised when You said, 'I will give you a new heart and put within you a right Spirit, and take away your heart of stone and give you a heart of flesh'* (Ezekiel 36:26). *Please do this for me right now and replace my mind with the mind of Christ so that I can think correctly.*

*"Please pour Your love into my heart as the Bible says You will do. And may Your love flow out to those around me as I move into the day because, Jesus, this is what You promised to do through those who believe in You.*

"Lord, I now ask that You put hostility between me and the things of the world and the flesh. And I ask that You implant within me a hunger for holiness and an appetite for righteousness.

"I also invite You to destroy every nerve and neuron that responds to snakebit thoughts, and I pray that You will install new nerve endings that are responsive to Your thoughts and to right actions.

*"Please micromanage my life today. You have said, 'Commit your way to the* Lord, *trust in Him'* (Psalm 37:5) *and He will act. I choose right now to commit my way to You and claim that promise, eagerly looking forward to Your divine involvement and intervention in my life today.*

*"Lord, I am aware that my situation apart from You is desperate and hopeless. But I am reminded that Jesus promised, 'I have given you power over...all the power of the enemy'* (Luke 10:19) *and that "nothing will be impossible for you'* (Matthew 17:20). *So now I claim these promises and thank You, Lord, that so equipped and empowered, I can fulfill Your instruction to the first disciples to become one of heaven's healing agents down here in the war zone. Please increase my faith as I choose to receive Your words.*

*"Lord, may Your love now flow through me in a healing stream of loving words and actions to those around me as I move into the day.*

*"Thank You for emptying me of self today and recreating within me a new self created to be like You in true righteousness and holiness. Please enable the new me to become more and more like You in character and in conduct.*

*"I ask these things in the wonderful name of Jesus, who promised, 'My Father will give you whatever you ask in my name'"* (John 16:23).

## Important Note

Praying this kind of prayer may seem a bit ho-hum after a few days. But the danger of not doing this is that your original self will return to life. An alive self allows our worst thoughts and addictions to dominate us once again. But a dead self brings God's resurrection power into our life so that we can increasingly become more like Jesus and also get our needs met. Keep in mind that your original, corrupted self can never be satisfied.

# An Overview of Grace

Grace is an amazing attribute of God that He offers to human beings who need it desperately. You can know grace is occurring if you're okay when you shouldn't be. Like when you're being unjustly criticized and don't defend yourself even if you're pretty sure you're right. Here are some definitions and quotations about grace to help you understand it better:

## A Dictionary Definition

The influence of the Spirit of God operating in humans to regenerate or strengthen them. Mercy, clemency, pardon. An act of grace. Moral strength.—*Webster's Unabridged Dictionary*.

## A Theological Definition

The freely given and unmerited favor of God.

## Two Bible Definitions

*"For by grace you have been saved through faith; and this is not your own doing, it is the gift of God, not because of works, lest anyone should boast"* (Ephesians 2:8).

*"My grace is sufficient for you, for My power is made perfect in weakness"* (2 Corinthians 12:9).

## Some Purposes of Grace

The tendencies that control the snakebit self (selfishness, tendency to criticize, nasty disposition, depression, addictions, pornographic thinking, et al) can be subdued by regular infusions of grace.

"When we yield ourselves as instruments for the Holy Spirit's working, the grace of God works in us (1) to deny old inclinations, (2) to overcome powerful propensities, and (3) to form new habits" (From *Christ's Object Lessons,* p. 354).

## How to Receive Grace

*"He [God] gives grace to the humble"* (Proverbs 3:34).

*"Let us then approach the throne of God with confidence, so that we may receive mercy and find grace to help us in our time of need"* (Hebrews 4:16).

## For Your Reflection

"The masterful passions of the heart no human can control. We are as helpless as were the disciples to calm the raging storm (that almost drowned them).... However fierce the tempest, those who turn to Jesus will find deliverance. His grace, which reconciles us to God, quiets the strife of human passion, and in His love the heart is at rest" (Christian author Ellen G. White).

Regular infusions of grace neutralize our snakebitness and can transform relationships. Ingest as often as needed. Grace will help you be kind, loving, and patient when you would prefer to be otherwise. And God never runs out.

## A Prayer for Grace

"Father in Heaven, I ask that You anoint my entire being with the oil of Your divine grace. I choose to place every molecule and neuron of my being—my mind, my heart, my imagination—under the authority and control of the Holy Spirit. As You infuse Your grace into my life today, please enable me to become a kinder, sweeter, more gracious person, more like Jesus in character and in conduct, I ask in His holy name. Amen."

# Messages From Jesus to You

*"I will betroth you to Myself forever;*
*betroth you to Myself*
*in lawful wedlock,*
*with unfailing devotion and love.*
*I will betroth you to Myself*
*to have and to hold,*
*and you shall know the Lord."*
—Hosea 2:19, 20

*"I will dwell in them*
*and walk in them;*
*and I will be their God,*
*and they will be My people."*
—2 Corinthians 6:16

*"You will seek Me and find Me*
*when you search for Me*
*with all your heart.*
*I will be found by you."*
—Jeremiah 29:13

Made in the USA
San Bernardino, CA
31 May 2014